ENGLISH PRONUNCIATION, INTONATION AND ACCENT REDUCTION — FOR RUSSIAN SPEAKERS

PEGGY THARPE

Copyright © 2019 by Peggy A. Tharpe

Content Editor: Gina Mathis

Copy Editor: Carolyn Kernberger

All rights reserved.

This book or any portion thereof may not be reproduced or used in any manner whatsoever without the express written permission of the author except for the use of brief quotations in a book review.

Printed in the United States of America

First Printing, 2019

The URL addresses referenced in this book were live and correct at the time of publishing. All websites were functioning at the time of this book's publication, but this may be subject to change.

Requests for permission to use should be directed to peggy@AmericanPronunciationCoach.com

Until we learn to do otherwise

We hear with our first language ears

Speak with our first language tongues

And communicate with our first language code.

Peggy Tharpe

CONTENTS

READ BEFORE BUYING   vii

Part 1 GETTING READY   1

Part 2 VOWELS   17

Part 3 CONSONANTS   65

Part 4 INTONATION AND PITCH   103

Part 5 WELL DONE!   137

READ BEFORE BUYING

Hello dear readers!

This is a book by a pronunciation teacher, for teachers and advanced students of English. It has many links to resources and recordings and practice activities.

The links are live in the e-book, but if you are buying the print version, live website links are provided on a private webpage. The URL and password you will need to view that private webpage are at the end of the book, on the *Also By Peggy Tharpe* page. Before you begin, go to that page and sign in to the webpage so you will be ready.

I apologize for the inconvenience.

My recordings will always be here, but I can't guarantee that the outside resources will be, because they were created by other people. So use them now and learn what you can while they are still up and running!

Happy Trails and Happy Teaching.

See you inside!

Peggy Tharpe

PART 1 GETTING READY

I know you are ready to jump into this pronunciation project and start work, but before we do that, I want to share some things that will make your studies go more smoothly. Let's talk about finding the resources I will refer to, the symbols I will use, and a few things that have a significant effect on your sound in English.

This section, Part 1, is the getting-ready section—our meeting of the minds. We will launch into crazy-hard-but-totally-worth-it practice in Parts 2, 3, and 4.

1

SYMBOLS AND DICTIONARIES

WE CAN'T SIMPLY USE English letters to talk about English sounds because there is no exact one-to-one correlation. The spelled A, for example, can make the Ã sound you hear in the word *date*, the Æ sound' in *bat*, the AH sound like *father*, or the AW sound in *daughter*.

Looking at it the other way, from sounds to spellings, the ā sound heard in *day* can be spelled in various ways: *date, weight, hay, nail* or *bouquet*. This is true for other English sounds, also.

Therefore, you and I must come to an agreement about symbols and sounds before we begin our discussion.

Over the decades, many phonetic symbol systems have been created. I know of at least eight. They are all referred to IPAs— International Phonetic Alphabets. IPAs are systems originally designed by and for linguists to identify and catalog all the sounds made in all the world's languages. But IPAs are unnecessarily complicated and confusing as a study tool. And there is no new, leaner system that everyone agrees on.

Many teachers still use the old IPA, while others, like myself, have created their own simplified system. I'll be using a simplified set of symbols. On the next page are the symbols I will use for English sounds while we work together.

VOWELS

bait	ā	beat	ē
hot, bot	ä	put, book	ü
bit	ɪ	bought	ɔ
boat	ō	bat	æ
boot	ū	bet	ɛ
but, butt	ə	girl, diver	ɚ ɝ

CONSONANTS   th in thin θ   th in that ð

IMPORTANT NOTE ABOUT SYMBOLS USED

Most of the symbols I use are for vowel sounds because English doesn't have a strong correlation between vowel spelling and vowel pronunciation. You may see me comparing sounds with æ or ō or ə symbols. And sometimes I'll use letters to indicate sounds, for example UH and AH. I use what helps me communicate the easiest to you, and hopefully, it isn't confusing.

English consonants have a closer one-to-one relationship between letter and sound than vowel sounds, so I use fewer consonant symbols, however we *will* use two differing symbols for TH because there are two possible sounds. American English is a living language, though, and native speakers are gradually changing their TH use. We'll talk about that later.

BEFORE YOU BEGIN, PLEASE DO THIS

First check your online dictionary and your other pronunciation tools and resources to determine what symbols they use. During our time together, I want you to use Merriam-Webster for your online dictionary: m-w.com. M-W and I differ slightly on a few symbols, but the pronunciation recordings are in American English, and that's important for you.

M-W has several dictionaries and thesauri on their website. If you feel that the definitions and examples in the homepage dictionary are too difficult, switch to M-W's ESL/EFL dictionary where the definitions are more clear and more examples of the word in context are provided.

2

WELCOME

HOW THIS GUIDE IS ORGANIZED

IT'S SO nice to have you join me. My name is Peggy Tharpe. I am an accent reduction and English fluency coach, and a lifetime ESL/EFL teacher.

I've written this book for Russian students of English and their teachers, tutors, and coaches. It covers the issues that I work on the most, and the strategies I use the most, with my high-intermediate and advanced level students to improve their sound in English. If you'd like to know more about me, you'll find a link to it in Chapter 2 on the private webpage.

If you are a teacher or tutor, please note that from this point on, I will be using 'you' to address a Russian student of English, rather than a teacher. It's just easier this way. Since you are a teacher, coach or tutor, I know you can adapt, because that's what we do, right?

* * *

When it comes to the sounds of Russian and English, we have a lot in common. In this guide, we will concentrate on big areas we don't have in common, and little areas that all English learners have to work on.

We're going to:

- Discuss how your first language affects your pronunciation of English
- Talk about how our *modes* of speaking differ and learn the English mode
- Add some missing vowels and change a few consonants
- Modify your word stress patterns to sound more like a native speaker of English
- Learn how pitch change differs in Russian and English
- Learn how intonation patterns differ in Russian and English
- Strengthen your ownership of the sound of English

THIS GUIDE HAS 4 PARTS

PART 1 compares English and Russian **sound systems**. If you are a student of English and find Part 1 difficult to understand, go to Part 2 and start working on your vowels. But please come back to Part 1 because it's full of important information that you need to know. Part 1 also tells what symbols and materials we will use throughout this guide.

PART 2 is all about the 'construction materials' you need to create your English sound—**vowels**. You'll learn why they are hard to change and what you need to do differently to gain control over these 'raw materials' so you can speak with a more natural stress, rhythm, and intonation.

PART 3 addresses your other 'building materials'—**consonant sounds**. You'll find lots of practice activities to help you change these critical markers needed by your listeners to recognize the words you are saying.

PART 4 is *extremely* important for you as a native Russian speaker. We will talk about what you must do to dispel confusion regarding your intentions and attitudes. Part 4 covers **pitch and tone**, which make a huge difference in how your message is received by English native speakers and is quite different between Russian and English. Tone is very important in English, more than you can imagine. Tone use strongly affects how people perceive you and interpret what you've said.

PART 5 is where we say good-bye, exchange numbers, and promise to keep in touch!

3

SPECIAL SYMBOLS IN CHAPTER HEADINGS

SOME OF THE challenges you face are challenges for *everyone* learning English pronunciation. Others are like Russian flags waving at your listeners, telling them that *Russian* is definitely your first language. When you see these flags ▶ ▶ in a chapter title, it signals something that identifies you as Russian.

If you see this 🎧 at the beginning of a chapter, it means there are recorded practice materials or study activities on the internet. Remember, if you bought the print edition, you'll find all these on the private webpage listed in the 'Also By Peggy Tharpe' page at the back of this book.

4

MATERIALS WE WILL USE 🎧

BOOKMARK THESE WEBSITES NOW

THIS BOOK IS rich in resources and learning strategies.

This is your last reminder, kids! I will be sending you to websites and recordings to complete practice exercises, so you must have access to the internet. The links are live in the ebook, but if you are a reading this in print, these website links are on a private webpage, and the keys to that webpage are at the end of the book, on the *Also By Peggy Tharpe* page. (Ebook readers are welcome to use the private webpage also.)

* * *

Your first assignment is to bookmark the websites below, right now, so you can easily find them. Mobile versions of these sites may not have all the features I'll be talking about, so you may have a richer experience if you use a laptop or computer.

* * *

Sounds of Speech by the University of Iowa, will help you understand the building blocks of English sound, vowels and consonants. It's a free website, and I will be sending you here often for study and practice. There is also an app for your phone, but it's not free and may look different. Unfortunately, Sounds of Speech relies on Flash Player, the website is set to be retired at the end of December, 2020. If you appreciate it as much as I do, please take a moment and petition the ESL Director to keep it going: maureen-burke@uiowa.edu. If there were a lot of other sites like this, it wouldn't matter so much, but I haven't seen another website with all this information organized in such a helpful way. If you're reading this post-2020, it means advocates and fans of the site, like me, weren't able to persuade the University of Iowa to invest in it further. Please join us.

Many Things is a great website created by Charles Kelly. It has lots of listening exercises and other information. Most of the time, we will use manythings.org/pp. Look around the manythings.org website; there are a lot of useful materials there.

Playphrase.me is a website with tons of video clips taken from British and American movies. We will use them in Part 4 to help you become familiar with how native speakers use intonation and pitch to shape common phrases. You're going to love this!!!!

Merriam-Webster Online Dictionary, m-w.com. This is an American English online dictionary that uses a shorter set of symbols for English than the IPA, which is more traditional and unnecessarily complicated. M-W (Merriam-Webster) uses symbols similar to mine. I want you to use this website instead of the one you are using now. We'll be working on American English sounds, so it's important to hear American English speakers.

EnglishClub.com is a free online English learning website. We will use their exercises selectively because it is a British site and certain sounds are different in British and American.

Train Your Accent is an offshoot of Randall's ESL Cyber Listening Lab, an online website. These listening activities will help you hear and practice the use of schwa as a reduced vowel in unimportant words. This will improve your rhythm and word stress.

My YouTube Channel. I will occasionally send you here to watch a video about a topic we are studying.

Bookmark the above websites now and look them over before we begin.

PART 2 VOWELS

Many small English words differ from each other only by their vowel sound: *bit, bet, bat, but, bot, boot, bite, bait, bought.* Developing and mastering all the English vowel sounds definitely will help with your Russian accent. We will work on this in Part 2.

BUT vowels have other very important jobs in English. And Russian speakers need a crash course in those roles, as well. Vowels play an active, vital role in stress and rhythm, which are needed by native listeners so they can follow your ideas. Native speakers lengthen and strengthen vowels to structure both syllable stress and word stress.

Still another way that vowels play a critical role is in supporting intonation curves. Native speakers lengthen the vowels so that they can bend the sound over the tops of intonation hills. More about this in Part 4.

5

SURPRISING CONTRIBUTORS TO ACCENT

AND WHAT YOU CAN DO ABOUT THEM

LET TALK about some contributors to your Russian sound in English that you may not have considered. If you want to sound more like a native speaker in American English, you must learn how to hold your jaw and mouth in an American way.

HOW TO HOLD YOUR JAW

Let's begin with your jaw. When you speak in Russian, your lower jaw sits a bit higher and closer to your upper jaw than it should for English. This closeness creates a smaller oral cavity, which is perfect for Russian, but many American English vowels require a looser, *lower* jaw to create a large mouth space, sometimes in the back of the mouth.

Here's how I think of it—Russian needs a **tunnel** between the upper and lower jaws for your tongue to move forward and backward. The lower jaw stays consistently close to the upper jaw, especially in the back, and tongue movements are short and quick because the small space inside the mouth limits how much the tongue can move.

English often needs a loose jaw that hangs low in a neutral, relaxed position. This is the natural resting state in American English and from here you can do either of the following:

- You can make a bigger open cave-like space by disengaging your jaw even more for big English vowel sounds like ō, ä, æ, aow, aiy, and uh which require a more space and time to develop.
- Or you can close your jaws so your tongue can quickly reach consonant sounds like T, D, L, N, S, ER, K, G, and tense vowel sounds like ā and ē. I call this position 'The Butterfly' and we'll talk about the Butterfly in Part 2 of this guide.

There's more up and down action in English; more forward and backward action in Russian.

NEUTRAL JAW POSITION

Find a clean pencil and hold it gently in your mouth between your teeth. Let your face and jaw and lips be as relaxed as possible. Hold the pencil loosely so it wobbles as you balance it between your teeth. Let your facial muscles relax, with loose lips and no pressure on the pencil; just balance it there between your teeth. This is the distance that you should have between your upper and lower teeth most of the time. This pencil trick helps you feel how relaxed your jaw should be, and how far apart.

Now try talking with the pencil in your mouth! Yes, the pencil will be in the way of some tongue movements, but even with it there and in the way, you will be able to speak English with a space between your upper and lower jaw, and you will sound much more like a native speaker (except for times when the pencil is obstructing your articulation)!

Now take the pencil out, but let your jaws hang loosely with about that much pencil-space between them.

By keeping your jaw loose and ready in neutral position, you can quickly lower it more to make the big-space sounds like O, AOW, AH and UH. And from this loose neutral position, you are also ready to make that most common sound in English, the schwa, which is the key to English word pronunciation, stress, rhythm and intonation.

Remember: The most important practice to do before you begin speaking in English is to relax, relax, relax your jaw, tongue and lips. Keep your jaw loose and low, with that gap between your upper and lower teeth. I know...I've said it at least 100 times. Are you getting my message?

JAW EXERCISES

Do the following exercises to loosen and relax your jaw. Always do this before you begin speaking in English, especially if you've been speaking Russian just before.

1. Widen and open your jaw as much as possible, really stretching it open, then relax everything—your mouth, your jaw, your tongue. Repeat.
2. Let your lower jaw disengage at the back so it hangs low and loosely. Move your lower jaw to the left and right, back and forth. This low position is very important for certain big vowel sounds. Stay relaxed as you do this left-right movement.
3. The ä/ah sound is made with the jaw low and relaxed and it needs a big, loose starting position! Imagine you are at the doctor's office and the doctor is flattening your tongue with a tongue depressor. Do you feel how big your mouth opening is? When your jaw is lowered like this, and also relaxed, you are in good position to say ä, the sound in *hot*, *pot*, and *father*.
4. uh/ə is a critical English sound made with a loose jaw. When it is reduced to a small sound, it's called *schwa*. It's the underlined sound in the words *above, mother,* and *unhappy*. The schwa sound is the most relaxed and frequent sound made in English. It's made with vocal fold vibration in your throat—no tongue, no lips, no jaw moves.
5. To prepare for schwa, let your jaw relax and hang loosely. Let your tongue fall to the bottom of your mouth and just lie there

asleep. (Press down on the center of your tongue and hold your finger there until you feel your tongue muscles relax completely). Let your tongue lie there, relaxed, as air flows up from your lungs and passes over your vocal folds. Stay there and make a sighing sound—the kind of sound you make when you sit down after work and completely relax, letting air flow out of your mouth. This relaxed jaw position is the best way to form the underlined sound found in words like *above*, *mother*, and *unhappy*. You are practicing how to keep a relaxed jaw and say the most common sound in English!

TONGUE POSITION

When speaking Russian, the tongue's resting or neutral position is naturally higher than it is for English.

Imagine how your mouth would be shaped and would feel if you had a small ball resting in the middle of your tongue. Your jaw would be lower and your tongue would be curved underneath the ball. That's the shape to emulate for English.

Your tongue has lots of work to do in English. Your tongue must cover more vertical distance for English, because of the lower neutral jaw position we often use. Your tongue tip must be ready to leap upward to form S, SH, Z, T, D, N, L, TH, ER, and R. When one of these consonant sounds follow a vowel sound that requires a low open oral space, such as *four, fire, far, fury* you will have further to go with your tongue.

TONGUE EXERCISES

1. Stretch your tongue forward and out of your mouth, trying to touch your chin with the tip of your tongue. While you've got your tongue stretched out, say AE (the American vowel sound in *hat, and, dad*) and hold it for as long as you can. When you release it, let your jaw hang loosely and your tongue lie in the bottom of your mouth. This practice will help you get ready

for the AE sound. If you'd like to hear all the vowel and consonant sounds modeled correctly, go to Sounds of Speech and enjoy the interactive diagrams and modeled sounds. Here is a demonstration video that shows you how to navigate this website. The homepage has been changing frequently, but keep watching to see how the features work on the inside. I'll be sending you to this website a lot in this guide. (if you're reading this post-2020, the website *may* not exist anymore, but at the time of this writing, it's still the best tool around for understanding the system of English sounds).
2. Here's an important exercise to do! Raise your tongue until its "shoulders" or sides touch the insides of your upper molars. While holding your tongue in this position, curl the tip of your tongue up slightly, and then relax it. The tip of your tongue should float freely and move, while the "shoulders" of your tongue stay anchored at the upper molars. You'll need this for the ER sound. We'll talk about ER in its own chapter.
3. Let your tongue drop to the bottom of your mouth and rest there, flat and wide, with the center in a soft shallow cup-shape. Say 'uhhhhhhhhh.' Remember that ball held loosely in your mouth? Imagine your tongue lying curved underneath it. Then say 'uhhhhhh' from your vocal chords, and don't use your jaw or tongue. This is such an important exercise! You are going to need to feel comfortable in this tongue position to change your Russian 'ah' sound into English 'uh' and master reductions and rhythm, also.

YOUR LIPS

Russian uses more tense, compressed, vertical lips. English has a loose, relaxed jaw and tongue, resulting in loose lips. A lot of the action in English, especially American English, happens inside the mouth with loose jaw and lips.

LIP EXERCISES

These exercises will help you loosen up and get ready to speak English.

1. Loosen your jaw, which will loosen your lips. There should be a small gap between your upper and lower teeth as your lower jaw hangs loosely. Then make the sound "PUH, PUH, PUH" with a lot of air, relaxing your lips after each sound. This loose jaw and loose lips after saying "PUH" is the natural resting position for your lips in English. Then purse your lips like you're going to kiss a baby's forehead, make a P sound and continue with the vowel sound ū in the word '*you*'. Practice moving your pursed lips out as far as you can, then let them fall loosely after the ə sound in '*puh*', with your jaw hanging loosely. There should be a gap between your upper and lower teeth, for both sounds. Go back and forth between these two positions, with lips pursed for the ū sound, and relaxed and loose for ə. This will help you do 2 things: strengthen your upper lip muscle, and quickly fall into relaxed, neutral schwa. Repeat 15 times.
2. Here's another sequence to practice. Say UH with relaxed lips, jaw, and tongue, then say 'EEEE' with a wide smile. Then return to a relaxed UH (schwa) position. Go back and forth between these two sounds. Hold on to each sound and lengthen them. This will help you learn to lengthen your vowels. Quicken your pace so you can go quickly from tense to relaxed to tense. Repeat 15 times so these movements start to feel more natural.
3. Now practice all three movements: the smiling horizontal stretch, the pursing lips, and the resting position. Stretch your lips horizontally for ē and ā, purse your lips and push them forward for ū, then relax your lips for the ə resting position. Repeat 15 times.
4. Here's an exercise to help you round your lips more for W. With jaw and lips hanging loosely, disengage your jaw even

more—make a bigger space for this big sound—and begin the sound at the back. Pretend you have a ball in your mouth and make a sound that starts at the back of your mouth, fills up the space with a big, round, Ō sound. Imagine pulling your lips around the ball of sound and make a small, tight circle with your lips. As you close your lips, make a small W or U sound: 'ŌŌw' or 'ŌŌu', and say *toe, sew, no, though, go*. Hold each ō for a while. In one syllable words, this O vowel has a long duration. It's a big part of the information native listeners need to recognize the word you are saying. Repeat 15 times.
5. You need a mirror for the next exercise. Go to the Sounds of Speech website. As you practice the vowels and consonants in the remaining chapters of this guide, compare your lip, jaw, and tongue movements with the movements of the model. Exaggerate the movements as you practice so that it will show up in some small way when you're actually speaking in English. Practice each sound 15 times.

SUMMARY

- Always keep your lower jaw loose, with a resting gap between upper and lower teeth of about ¼ - ½ centimeter.
- Learn to let your tongue rest in the bottom of your mouth for schwa. Native speakers use this position and sound to conserve energy.
- Because your jaw is hanging loose, and your tongue is resting in the bottom of your mouth, most of the time your lips can be relaxed also. But not always. Certain sounds, like ER, benefits from pursing their lips and pushing them forward. We'll talk about this more in a later chapter.

6

VOWELS - THE HEART AND SOUL OF ENGLISH 🎧

OVERVIEW

ENGLISH HAS MORE vowel sounds than Russian, and it's likely you are using Russian **vowel** sounds for the English sounds that Russian doesn't have.

Doing this has several consequences. The most obvious is that it may actually change the meaning of the word, for example, *bat* vs. *bet*. (This æ vs. ɛ vowel mixup is common for Russian speakers.) English has quite a few one-syllable word pairs in which the vowel sound is the only difference. Occasionally these mispronunciations cause confusion, but for the most part, they only create your accent and signal your first language.

But there is another thing that happens with vowels. In English, **syllable stress** is created by adjusting the length, strength, energy level and pitch location of vowel and consonant sounds (mostly vowels). We lengthen and strengthen a word's stressed syllable vowel sound and pronounce it more clearly, while we shorten, weaken, even swallow unstressed vowels.

You know a bit about weakening vowels because you do it also in Russian—you articulate clear vowels in stressed syllables which causes a contrast between stressed and unstressed syllables. If you'd like to see what I'm talking about, watch this YouTube video about vowel stress in Russian.

Getting the stressed vowels to sound right will help your listeners immensely—they will be much better able to quickly catch the words and phrases of your message—so pay close attention to your English stressed vowel sounds.

Vowels also place a huge role in **intonation**. Intonation is the rise and fall of your voice as you speak. Your voice can rise and fall in pitch, making hills and valleys that rise and fall in energy also. This rising and falling in pitch and energy is something that native speakers often do simultaneously. Imagine a line that has hilltops and valleys, like this:

A speaker's voice can increase and decrease energy without pitch change also, which changes the sound from a melody to a rhythmic series of beats or pulses. Native speakers usually use all these tools at once, adjusting them as circumstances and mood require. But we are going to talk about pitch change because Russian and English use pitch differently.

In English, you should say new information (nouns and verbs, adverbs and adjectives) on the hilltops of this wavy line above. Your voice should smoothly glide upward on focus words and downward on functional words (grammatical words such as articles and prepositions). These rises and falls are not sharp or quick; they usually flow up and down smoothly. Quick pitch changes are reserved for dramatic expressions, and to mark the end of a sentence and the start of a new idea. But quick pitch changes are used in normal speech in Russian, so we will work on that in Part 4.

Learning to *lengthen* your stressed syllable vowels is very important. If you do this, it's easier to glide your words up and over the hilltops and down the hillsides of your intonation curves. Like Russian, English pitch change is used for stress. Unlike Russian, lengthening stressed syllables and words also signals stress. This combination of pitch rise/fall, plus lengthening of key syllables and words, tells listeners which words are most important in your message.

We will start with vowels because they take a lot of persistence and practice, but the benefits will come at the word level, the phrase level, and the sentence level.

Set up a regular practice time to review the vowels you have studied. *Always* review them, even when you start working on consonants and intonation. The more you practice lengthening and strengthening your vowel sounds, the more natural you'll sound and the easier it will be for you to control them. When you switch back to Russian, you will revert to your unconscious speech habits, so you must keep reminding your mind and your muscle memories about English sounds.

SUMMARY

- Mispronouncing vowels can cause confusion for listeners. Most of the time, the context of your conversation resolves possible confusions. This does, however, give you a strong accent.
- *Over*-pronouncing vowel sounds that should be small and weak, and *under*-pronouncing vowels that should be strong and long, makes your speech sound noticeably different. Knowing when and how to strengthen and weaken vowels is key.
- We stretch the vowel across the top of the intonation curve, gliding up and sliding down on the vowels. Without intonation curves, native listeners will have to work harder to understand your message.

7

▶ ▶ SEPARATE UH FROM AH 🎧

TO IMPROVE YOUR STRESS, RHYTHM AND INTONATION

I WILL USE UH, schwa, ʌ and ə to refer to the underlined sound heard in *b<u>u</u>tter* (UH) and *<u>a</u>live* (schwa or ə).

I will use AH to talk about the stressed syllable sound in *f<u>a</u>ther*, *c<u>o</u>ntract*, *t<u>o</u>p*.

UH is the **least constricted sound** in English. Its sound comes from gentle vibrations in your throat as air passes over the vocal folds. Your lips and tongue are completely relaxed, and your jaw hangs loose with a slight space between upper and lower teeth. Other English vowels require you to do something else in addition to vocalizing the sound, such as lowering your jaw, or reshaping your tongue. But not schwa! It's merely air passing over your vocal folds, making a sound in your throat as it passes.

UH is also the **most common sound** in English. It is everywhere. It's like a thread that holds together the fabric of English speech.

The sound UH is represented by two symbols in the IPA (International Phonetic Alphabet), but it is the same sound. The two symbols refer to the character of the sound—how much stress is given to the sound—and that depends on whether it occurs in the stressed syllable, /ʌ/, or the unstressed /ə/ syllable of a word.

As a Russian speaker of English, you probably replace UH with AH in words like b_utter, m_other, p_utty, d_oesn't, w_asn't, d_ummy, c_ousin. You may say butter as bah.ter, mother as mah.ther, and putty as potty. If you want to sound less Russian when you speak English, learn to use the UH sound (instead of AH) when UH it is called for in the stressed syllable.

On the other hand, when the UH sound is referred to as schwa, it occurs in unstressed syllables. This mini-sound is truly mighty. It creates stress contrast within words so listeners can recognize what you are saying, and it also helps to shape English rhythm and stress patterns. If you haven't learned to shrink and reduce unstressed vowels into small schwa sounds yet, you won't have a native-speaker stress and rhythm when you speak.

PRACTICE CHANGING AH TO UH

1. Hear the difference. First, make sure you can hear the difference between UH and AH in stressed position by playing this listening discrimination game. Go to http://www.manythings.org/pp and choose Lesson 21. Go through the listening exercise, choosing the sound you hear. Work toward a 90% or better score. The starting page looks like this.

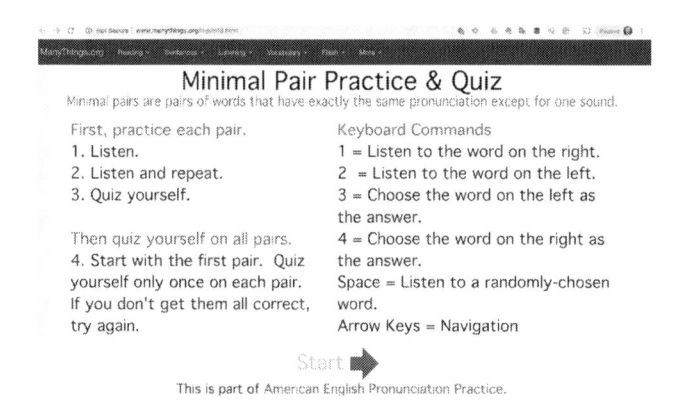

2. Learn the correct articulation of both sounds. To learn the correct way to say UH, compare Sounds of Speech website's interactive diagrams for /ʌ/ and /ə/, and watch the model. Then compare them to the vowel sound AH which is represented on their website with this symbol: /ɑ/ for AH. Imitate the model and repeat the examples for all three. You may have to repeat these exercises before you feel and hear the difference between the UH sounds and the AH.

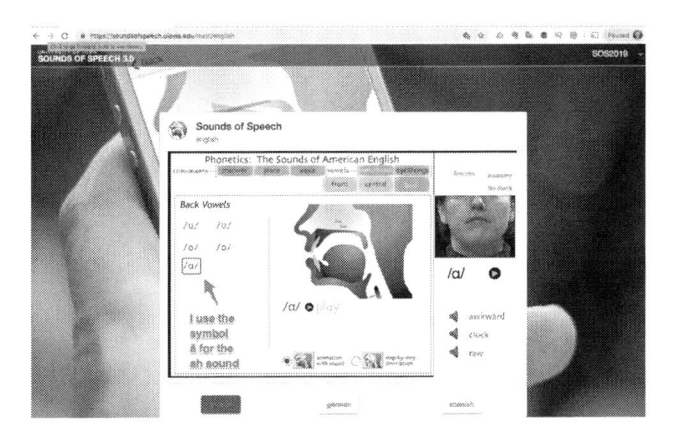

NOTE: The Sounds of Speech website uses two symbols for the UH sound in English: /ʌ/ and /ə/. The /ʌ/ represents UH in stressed position and /ə/ represents unstressed UH. They are the same sound, made in the same way. In active speech, the stressed UH is often longer and may be placed on a higher pitch, while the unstressed UH will be weak, short and lower in pitch. But they're the same vowel sound!

Your job is to study how the tongue, lips and jaw move for schwa—it is the same sound for both /ʌ/ and /ə/. Listen to them both and watch the model; you'll see that nothing changes in the sound or the movements.

In reality, only the energy and duration you give them will change based on whether they are stressed or unstressed.

Remember, schwa is a central vowel and it is completely relaxed. Just vibrate your vocal folds and let the sound come out of your loosely separated jaws.

3. Strengthen and separate the two sounds using minimal pairs.
'Minimal pairs' are two words that have only one sound that is differ-

ent, like *wine/vine, or pat/put.* They're a great way to practice learning to make the sounds you are having trouble with. You'll strengthen your muscles, learn to hear and feel the differences, and eventually develop unconscious habits.

Develop your muscle memories, create habits, and strengthen your command and control of the schwa sound by alternating back and forth between UH and AH in nearly identical words, for example *dug, dog.* Think of this step as 'going to the gym'—you must work out these new muscle movements and positions if you want schwa to become natural and comfortable and different from AH.

Here are some pairs to practice: the first word has UH, the second has AH. Keep the UH sound short with your jaw hanging loosely. Lengthen the AH sound and open your jaw more.

Remember, if you are reading the print version, recordings for word lists are on the private webpage and the access information is on the Also By *page at the end of this book.*

One syllable pairs: nut/not, pup/pop, what/watt, stuck/stock, but/bot, done/Don, up/op, un-/on, sub/sob, gulf/golf, bucks/box, duck/dock, luck/lock, shut/shot, gut/got, crutch/crotch

Multi-syllable pairs: rubber/robber, cuddle/coddle, tummy/Tommy, buddy/body, sputter/spotter, putter/potter, muddle/model, bussing/bossing.

If you don't feel or hear the difference between UH and AH, stay here and repeat Steps 1 and 2, then keep returning to it and practicing. Focus on creating the sounds differently and recognizing when you have done so. Alternating the sounds, back and forth, will build strength with the articulations and make you more comfortable with their differences.

4. UH sound in stressed syllables. Practice words that have schwa in the stressed syllable. Since you already know the AH sound, you need to rewire your brain to make new neural pathways for the schwa sound and ensure it becomes automatic."

You already know the AH sound. We have to rewire your brain now to make the pathways to and from UH more automatic. The internet has many pronunciation words lists for the schwa/uh (ə/ʌ) sound; a quick search will get you more lists.

Using Russian AH for English UH is most noticeable in words where the UH sound is stressed. Here is a starter list of common words with the UH sound stressed in the first syllable. Practice these!

mother, brother, other, under, double, money, shovel, lovely, lover, Monday, couple, hungry, customs, dustbin, wonderful, something, nothing, cousin, dozen, sudden, London, Russia, lovely, honey, someone.

Make sure your stressed syllables are longer than your unstressed syllables. Your stressed syllable in these words is a large part of the word's total duration. Use a 70%-30% ratio for syllable length in this list and be sure that you don't let your stressed syllable vowel sound (UH) become an AH sound.

5. UH sound shrinks in unstressed words. Even though Russian does reduce unstressed vowels, here is some practice to make sure you understand when to do it in English. Go to Train Your Accent, find the Oral Readings, and choose a topic you are interested in (for example, *Exercise and Fitness*). You'll see and hear which vowel sounds are reduced to schwa by the speaker. Listen to the energy flow and pitch of the speaker's voice. Listen as the speaker relaxes on unstressed syllables that have schwa. Then practice silently, out loud, along with him. Finally, play a short section and repeat it.

He does speak very quickly, so if you find his speed overwhelming, don't try to duplicate what he's saying. Instead, relax and listen to the sounds of his voice, noting energy and pitch changes, and the words and sounds that are reduced. Think about why. The more you listen to the passage, the more you'll begin to understand his words, and eventually, it won't seem as fast. Native listeners don't expect *you* to speak this quickly. Many native speakers themselves don't speak this fast. We may speak slowly. We may speak quickly. We adjust our pace to meet our conversational circumstances.

Don't jump from passage to passage; instead, study the same one over and over until you feel comfortable with the sounds of the words and the rhythm of the phrases.

The more you listen to the flow and rhythm of English, and then practice and imitate it, the easier it will be to understand native speakers and be understood by them.

6. The silent approach. Practice silently. This technique works very well for *some* of my students. Listen to a recording—anyone speaking slowly enough for you to follow—over and over, **silently** mouthing the words as the speaker says them. In the beginning, don't make any sounds, just silently say the words and silently apply the same stress, energy, duration and intonation changes to your own silent voice. Silently emphasize the stressed syllables, and silently relax your jaw on unstressed syllables. Think about how your tongue should be resting on the bottom of your mouth, relaxed, for all the schwa sounds. Practice all those things **silently** so you can feel how you make them, before you add sound.

7. Personalize your list. Make your own list of sentences with the UH words you often use when you speak. Let's say you want to work on the word *just* so you don't sound like you're saying *jahst*. To collect sentences with the word *"just"*, type http://www.manythings.org/sentences/words/just/ into your search bar (remember, if you're reading this in print, the link is on your web page of recordings). You should see 108 pages of sentences that have the word *just* in them. The first pages have sentences that are short, but they gradually get longer and more complex as you scroll through the pages.

As you can see from the audio symbols before the sentences, Pages 1 through 50 are recorded, but the rest of the sentences are not. Listen and practice, keeping in mind what you are trying to change—AH to UH. I'm joking a little bit about how much to practice, but you must remember that changing muscle memories requires a lot of repetition. A lot. You don't have to do it all at once and you don't have to do it for long periods of time, but keep working at words that have UH in the stressed syllable.

To work on a different word, like *mother*, use the same URL as above, but change the last part from /just/ to /mother/. To collect sentences with another word, for example '*mother,*' remove the last word, /just/ from the above URL and replace it with /mother/. This will take you to pages of sentences containing *mother*. Continue this cut-and-replace strategy for each word you want to practice in sentences.

Practice makes perfect, and practice makes permanent.

SUMMARY

- Both UH and AH require a low, loose jaw and a bigger oral cavity than is normal for Russian. But AH requires an intentionally lowered jaw, while UH has no movement or tension at all, and your jaws hang loosely apart. This makes them recognizably different to native speakers.
- UH can be a stressed sound in words like *butter, mother, cousin*. Russians tend to over-pronounce UH and say AH instead, which is a bigger and longer sound. If you use AH instead of UH, you'll say *bahter, mahther and cahzen*, a signal of your Russian roots.
- Unstressed UH is shorter, softer, and less clear. Reduced vowels help to highlight nearby stressed syllables, which makes the word easier for listeners to quickly recognize by its pattern of contrasting stress.
- Most unstressed vowels are reduced. One exception is ēē in final position, in words like *happy* or *worry*. Keep the length, but don't give them energy or stress.

8

SEPARATE THE VOWELS IN BIT AND BEAT

THIS PAIR OF SOUNDS IS A CHALLENGE FOR EVERYONE LEARNING ENGLISH

WE WILL USE the symbol ɪ for the short i sound in *bit*.

We will use the symbol ē for the long, tense vowel in *beat*. This ē sound in *beat* is also represented by the following symbols in other resources: i:, iy, and i. Sounds of Speech, where I want you to go right now, uses /i/. Find these two sounds heard in *beat* and *bit*, study how they're made, watch the model's jaw and lips, and note which symbols are used for these two sounds on Sounds of Speech and your favorite dictionary.

HIZ VS HEEZ

You may be mixing ē and ɪ sounds.

ē is a long, tense, forward sound made by stretching your lips sideways and pushing your tongue upward and forward into the space behind your front upper teeth. ē usually has a long duration—it takes longer to pronounce than ɪ does. Your tongue will press forward and the sides of your tongue will touch the inside of your upper molars.

For words that have the ē sound <u>at the end</u>, like *happily* or *Mary,* be careful not to clip the final ē too short. It shouldn't be stressed or strong, but it is probably longer than you think.

Meet has ē in the middle of the word. This middle ē should be tense and long between the m and the t, much longer than you think. It will feel unnatural, but this length and tension helps listeners recognize that you aren't saying *mitt* or *met*.

ɪ is completely different. It is relaxed and made in the center of the mouth. Start with your tongue lying relaxed in the bottom of your mouth, then raise the back half of your tongue briefly as you make the ɪ sound, pressing your tongue sides against the insides of your back molar teeth gently. Then release your tongue back down into neutral schwa position, or on toward the next consonant.

Many English learners substitute ē for ɪ. It doesn't tell listeners that you are Russian but it does flag you as someone whose first language isn't English. It's easily noticed by native speakers. The context of your conversation will probably resolve possible confusion for listeners.

BIT AND BYIT

Depending on where in Russia you are from, you may make a 'y' sound before the vowel, causing the word *his* to sound like *hyiz,* and *bit* to sound like *byit*.

Try this strategy to remove the 'y'. When you say *bit*, don't push your tongue forward on the vowel sound. Instead, loosen and drop your jaw before you begin the word. Pull your lips together over your teeth for 'b', then gently release them as you say the vowel sound.

Use the same technique for *knit* and *net*.

PRACTICE

This process is the same one you used for separating AH and schwa in the previous chapter.

Make sure you can **hear** the difference. Go to Manythings.org/pp and listen to Lesson 23.

Go to Sounds of Speech and study how the tongue, lips and jaw move differently for these two sounds, and how ē is longer and tenser, while ɪ is relaxed and often shorter. Practice imitating the model as she says both. Use your mirror and make sure your sounds are different from each other and your movements are like hers.

Strengthen your command and control of these two sounds by practicing the pronunciation of minimal pairs of words. On the website below you'll find minimal pairs to practice. Caution! EnglishClub uses the symbol /i:/ or /i/ for the ē sound, but I use the symbol ē. I don't want you to get confused. EnglishClub uses British pronunciations so sometimes I won't recommend it to you, but for these 2 sounds, ē and ɪ, British and American pronunciations are the same: https://www.englishclub.com/pronunciation/minimal-pairs-i-ee.htm

Think of a word with short i that you use a lot. Then use the method I showed you in the previous chapter (practice #7) to collect sentences having that word. As you practice saying these words and sentences, pay attention to the way you are pronouncing this sound. Remember, your lips and jaw should be totally relaxed for ɪ, but for ē, you should widen and tense your lips and push your tongue forward and upward with energy.

SUMMARY

- You may be using the ē sound in place of the ɪ sound, pronouncing short ɪ words like *hit, bit, simple* as *heat, beat* and *seemple* because of the tense vowel you are using. The i sound that you want to use is above schwa.
- Or you may be transposing the two sounds, so that ē is used in words like *sit* that require an ɪ sound, and ɪ is used in words like *seat*, that should have the ē sound.
- ē is very tense, very forward and upward, and has a long

duration. ɪ is made in the center of the mouth, is relaxed and very much like a schwa with a small upward movement of the center/back section of the tongue.
- If you are putting a little Y sound before vowels, saying *byit* instead of *bit*, open and loosen your jaws and don't push forward with your tongue when you say the vowel sound.

9

▶ ▶ DEVELOP YOUR AMERICAN Æ 🎧

/EH/ IS NOT LONG ENOUGH OR STRONG ENOUGH

WE WILL USE the symbol æ to represent the vowel sound in the word *bat*. We will use ɛ or EH for the vowel sound in *bet*.

Look up these two words, *bet* and *bat*, on Merriam-Webster.com and listen to how they are pronounced. Then compare the two vowel sounds on Sounds of Speech, represented by these symbols, æ and ɛ, and watch the articulation movements in the interactive diagrams.

Russian doesn't have the æ sound, so unless you have worked hard on this, you are probably using EH instead, which will give you a distinctly Russian sound in English.

The æ sound is important for you to acquire, both to sound more natural and to reduce your accent. It nearly always occurs in a stressed syllable, and it is longer, stronger, and more articulated than the EH sound you are more familiar with.

I'm repeating myself now, but for a good reason. Spoken English relies heavily on stress to shape words, so the vowel in a word's stressed syllable should be clearly recognizable. Make sure you pronounce stressed vowels with energy and clarity and more length.

Here's how to grow an American æ sound.

The æ sound is bigger, stronger, longer, more tense than ɛ. It is made with the jaw held much lower than for ɛ. This creates a bigger open space in your mouth for the sound to exit, making this a very forward, big sound.

Relax and loosen your jaw, and then lower it still further in front, pressing down on the back of your tongue also. Bring the sound forward through your open throat and lips and let it finish outside your mouth. Don't let it go up through your nose and become nasal.

If you're sounding nasal, try this experiment. Pinch your nose and experiment with how to make the æ sound come up from your lungs and throat and out your mouth, while blocking its passage through your nose. Most of the American AE sound comes from vibrations in your open throat, rather than your mouth. You will probably have to press down a bit on the back of your tongue to make the space open enough.

EH is shorter than æ. EH is made with your jaws closer together. EH isn't a big sound. It's made inside your mouth. If you can say the æ sound by itself, hooray! Just make sure you spend enough time on it when you are speaking so that it fully develops and doesn't get clipped short into an EH sound.

PRACTICE EXERCISES

1. Let's find out if you can **hear** the difference between æ and ɛ. Go to manythings.org/pp and play Lesson 7 to hear the difference between ɛ and æ. Keep working on this until you get 90% right. You've got to start hearing how the two sounds are different so you can begin making them differently when you speak.
2. Make sure you know how to **make** the 2 sounds. Watch the Sounds of Speech interactive diagrams. Notice how much stronger and longer æ is than ɛ. Use your mirror and make

sure your jaw and lip movements match those of the model. She exaggerates a bit, but it's a good place to start. You can relax later once you know how the sound should feel when you say it.
3. Try this trick. Begin by making the EH sound. Say it continuously, and while you are saying it, lower your jaw further and further and let your tongue more downward with your jaw. Push a bit on the back of your tongue. Did ɛ change to æ? For many people, it does.
4. Learn to **feel** what's different. Your tongue plays an important part in the æ sound. First open your jaws so they are loose and you have a wide, relaxed gap between your teeth. Then press the back of your tongue down to make a bigger space for the sound to exit. If that doesn't work, try pushing the back of your tongue forward with your jaw lowered in the front.
5. Record yourself and **evaluate** your sound compared to the model's on Sounds of Speech. Experimentation will help you become more comfortable making this very forward, very tense sound. Keep playing around with your mouth, your tongue and your jaw, making noises, and recording yourself. Don't give up. You need to hear it, feel it, and use it. That's a lot of changes. Practice will make it come to you.
6. Next, learn to **control** the two sounds and choose when to use them. There are two things to work on: 1) becoming aware of the longer duration of æ and shorter duration of ɛ; and 2) the lower jaw position of æ, which allows the sound to exit the mouth through a bigger space. Practice these minimal pairs often. Practice until you don't have to work so hard at making them differently and they come out more naturally. Get used to the æ sound by practicing these words every day until they come out of your mouth easily and comfortably.
7. Repeat these words as you listen to the recording: *add, that, as, at, have, had, can, an, back, after, man, ask, land, hand, animal, answer, last, example, began, family, stand, black, happened, fast, passed, pattern, plan, fact, class, ran,*

understanding, language, can't, matter, perhaps, dance, sat, past, happy, glass, paragraph, catch, gas, grass, valley, bad, practice, captain, capture, rather, value, branch, hat, cattle, Japanese, capital, factory, chance, triangle, France, actually, adjective, match, apple, track, scan

8. Read and practice these academic and business words as you listen to the linked recording: *analysis, contract, establish, factor, aspect, category, chapter, evaluate, impact, strategy, transfer, interaction, maximum, task, access, adequate, annual, attitudes, grant, parameter, status, academic, challenge, contact, transition, whereas, abstract, accurate, aggregate, allocation, attached, enhanced, transformation, transport, adapt, adaptation, advocate, channel, classical, dynamic, extract, transmission, abandon, ambiguous, dramatic, radical, random, analogous, anticipated, format, manual, overlap, relax, panel, antagonize, astronomical*

9. Choose an æ word you use often, like *ask*. Go through the following collection of sentences having the word *ask*. Practice by imitating the recorded sentences. Go to http://www.manythings.org/sentences/words/ask/. You'll see page after page of sentences with *ask* (some are recorded, some are not). If you are quite advanced in English, try some of the long sentences on the last pages! When you are ready to practice a different æ word, just change the end of the URL, i.e. remove "ask" from the end of the URL and insert whatever word you want to work on next.

SUMMARY

- Russian doesn't have the æ sound so you probably substitute EH for æ. Words like '*happy*' sound like *heppi* instead of *hæppēē*.
- æ is made with a bigger oral cavity, a lowered jaw and a depressed tongue. ɛ is made with a smaller jaw space, lips slightly pulled back at the corners, and the tongue pulled back.

- æ is longer and much more distinctly formed in the mouth. EH is a shorter sound and is more relaxed.
- æ usually occurs in stressed syllables, so if you can get this sound right, your syllable stress and word stress will improve.

10

LENGTHEN Ē, Ī, Ā, AND Ō 🎧

VOWEL LENGTH IS A STRESS STRATEGY IN ENGLISH

IF I COULD SAY this a million times to you, I would. **Lengthen the vowels in your stressed syllables when you speak English**. Don't force it. Just stay on the stressed vowel sound for a bit longer than you think feels natural.

You can also make vowels more energetic, or use a higher pitch, but you must learn to lengthen them by letting them vibrate in your throat for a while as they blend into the next sound. This lengthening will improve your word stress, rhythm, and intonation. This is a major key to improving your sound in English.

Vowel sounds in most other languages are shorter than English vowels. The problem for English learners is that the duration (length) they give to vowel sounds is an unconscious action—we instinctively use the tone lengths that we heard when we were listening to our mother's voice, in the womb. Before you were born, you were learning the rhythms of Russian. That's when you began learning about Russian's stress and intonation, and how it should sound. Needless to say, this is a very deep memory, and you may have to drill lengthening of vowel sounds so that you can begin to do that habitually.

PRACTICE

It's hard to remember to stay a little longer on the stressed vowels, and it's also hard to quantify and explain to you how to increase the energy or momentum of your stressed syllables. Fortunately, there's a solution that transcends explanations—the amazingly easy and highly effective **rubber band technique**! (I wish I knew who thought of this first so I could thank them.)

Cut a rubber band so it's a strip, hold an end in one hand, and stretch the other end out on the stressed syllable of a word, then release the rubber band quickly as you say the following, unstressed syllables. Watch me demonstrate this in a YouTube video I made. Make a list of the words you use often that have long vowel sounds like ē, ā and ī and ō There are also some word lists later in this chapter. Practice the words you need to say at least once a week with the rubber band to keep your muscle memories strong.

Use **body gestures**. Making a physical gesture helps you remember by building muscle memories, that certain vowels must be longer. Whether you use the rubber band, or devise movements or gestures of your own, like standing up or stretching out an arm, the idea is to find a way to remind your speaking muscles that you should be lengthening that vowel sound.

Over the years, as I taught and taught pronunciation, I developed a set of movements that work very well to help my clients remember the importance of duration in English vowels. They're difficult to explain in print but easy to demonstrate, so I made an online course on Udemy to show how to use your body to strengthen your English sounds.

Lengthen ā, ē, ī, ō, ū vowels in one-syllable words, using gestures or a rubber band. Then add multi-syllable words and stretch out on the stressed vowels. You can find many word lists online with a quick search. The website ontrackreading.com has one-syllable and multi-syllable words listed by vowel sound—get the pdfs for the 'second' vowels and use your rubber band or gestures to lengthen these stressed vowels.

Here are more long vowel words to practice.

1. All ē's are longer vowel sounds, whether stressed or unstressed. Stressed ones get more energy and, in two syllable words, a pitch change: *we, meter, weed, delete, meal, lead, yield, exceed, reason. Unstressed ē's get the same length, with less energy and sometimes a lower pitch: happy, lonely, hurry, messy, apology, anatomy*
2. Lengthen ī sounds, such as: *hi, hide, my, mine, file, files, filed, lie, lies, lied, Mike, assign, why, deny, reply, try, tried, dies, died, goodbye, fly, flies, cry, cries, cried, time, times, line, lining, lined, light, lights, ally, allies, size, sizes, realize, realized, decide, decided, hypothesize, emphasize, initialize, sympathize*
3. Lengthen ā sounds, whether they are in the stressed syllable or not: *hey, name, wait, strange, arranged, day, today, laid, mate, rate, hail, sane, lake, tame, same, blame, relate, today, Monday, Tuesday, Wednesday, Thursday, Friday, Saturday, Sunday*
4. Lengthen ō sounds: *no, know, note, notes, noted, hope, hopeful, float, floating, crow, clone, don't, won't, open, opening, below, zero, own, lower, solo, demo, drove, Pope, hoax, furlough, slope, known, antelope, revoke, revoked, slow, slowly, flowing, though, thrown, envelope, demote, demoted*
5. Lengthen ū sounds: *who, whom, food, rude, root, crude, blue, blues, two, zoo, true, loose, crew, brew, brewed, stews, stewed, shoot, shoe, shoes, roof, aloof, super, trooper, truthful, cruel, dutiful, sooner, new, renew, stool, rule, cruel, fruit, Tuesday, June, July*
6. Lengthen æ sounds: *ask, aspirin, has, hasn't, can't, apple, accident, attack, happen, map, rap, jazz, accent, ads, added, dazzling, rapid, antique, pants, advertise, accident, accurate, inaccurate, contract (verb + noun), impact (verb + noun), branch, plastic, bland, brand, ham, hamburger, romantic, Alaska, France*

SUMMARY

- Because Russian vowels are shorter in duration than American English vowels, you must learn to lengthen these tense, longer vowels of English.
- Rubber bands work well for practicing the long, tense English vowels. Stretch out the rubber band on the stressed vowel sounds. Even one-syllable words benefit from the rubber band.
- Gestures can also help you remember to lengthen your vowel sounds in stressed syllables of English. A stretch of the arm as you say the stressed syllable will help you remember to spend more time vocalizing the stressed vowel.

11

▶ ▶ AMERICAN ER SOUND 🎧

A BIG CHALLENGE—WITH A SURPRISING SOLUTION!

WE'LL DISCUSS the American ER sound first and talk about word-initial R in a following chapter. This makes it easier for you to learn both of them. Because the ER sound can have different spellings, I will represent the sound with ER and ɚ. The Sounds of Speech website's sideview diagrams don't help much for ER, but the model's lip movements are exactly what you should be doing, so have your mirror on hand, and be sure you can imitate her lip movements as we go through the following inside-the-mouth instructions.

NOTE: There are many, *many* word lists on the internet for your ER pronunciation practice. Be careful which you listen to because British and American use of R is quite different. I'm only going to tell you about American ER.

ALL ABOUT ER

American ER is very different from Russian R. Russian R is a high tap or flick of the tongue tip against the roof of the mouth. It requires no lip movements. In Russian, your tongue tip is high and your tongue back is low for the flick.

The American ER sound is **not** created by contacting the roof of your mouth with your tongue tip, as it is in Russian. American ER tongue position varies depending on what sound precedes it. In some words, like *hurry* or *urn,* your tongue is low before you begin ER. In others, like *sir* or *learn*, the tongue tip is high before the ER sound.

The ER sound is usually spelled with -ir, -er, -ur, -or, for example, *sir, her, hurry, worry,* but there are infrequent spellings of ER also, as in *learn.*

HOW TO MAKE A NATURAL ER SOUND

There are 3 physical positions for American ER. I call them the pitcher spout, the kiss, and the butterfly.

Part 1. The Pitcher Spout

OK…this will require a bit of imagination. I want you to imitate the shape of the spout of a pitcher with the front of your tongue (the spout is circled in the illustration above). Flute (curl up) the sides of your tongue *tip* into a shape like the spout of the pitcher above. Don't look at your tongue to do this; it won't help. Just curl the sides of your tongue tip so it feels like the spout above.

Imagine this sound as a liquid pouring forward down the valley along the middle of your tongue, from back to front, through the fluted front of your tongue and out through your extended lips. Next, get your lips into position!

Part 2. The Kiss

The Kiss helps you shape the ER sound as it exits your mouth. Imagine that you are going to kiss a baby; push your lips forward and form a small round opening. That is the position you want your lips to be in when you say ɚ. This will make the sound come forward and out through your lips and will help you avoid your R habit of flicking the roof of your mouth with your tongue tip. Study the Sounds of Speech model and watch the top of her upper lip closely—do you see the change in lighting as her upper lip moves forward?

Your current pronunciation of R is a habit that you learned and used your entire life; it doesn't require you to use your lips or keep your tongue low. But that's exactly what your English R needs.

Next, back to your tongue…the middle part.

Part 3. The Butterfly

The term 'Butterfly,' which I've seen attributed to Pam Marshalla, an American Speech and Language Pathologist, is the term I'll use for the tongue position that works best for the ER sound in English. Imagine the line made by following the tops of the butterfly's wings—high on the sides with a dip in the middle. This position makes the ER sound much easier to create and works very well when ER comes before or after sounds like T, S, or N. (These sounds are made up high in your mouth).

The aim of the Butterfly position is to anchor your tongue sides on the sides, while creating a dip in the middle. Here's how.

First, raise your tongue up and stretch out the sides of your tongue until they touch the insides of your upper molar teeth. Keep your tongue gently in contact with your molars.

Now that you are holding your tongue in the Butterfly Position with its sides anchored and its tip loose, notice what is happening to the middle of your tongue. There is a valley or dip in the middle. If we could look directly at your tongue from the front while it's in this position, we'd see a shape like the line along the top outline of a butterfly—it's also described as two hills with a valley in between.

Now think again about what is happening to the tip of your tongue. When you stretch the shoulders or sides of your tongue sideways to touch the molars, you shorten the length of your tongue, causing the tip to curl up a bit and move back a little. In this Butterfly position, make a pitcher spout shape with the tip, and hold your lips in the Kiss position. Now, with all that in place, say errrrrr!

PRACTICE

1. Practice this list of 1-syllable words with the ER sound. Follow along here as you listen to recording. *Word, worm, world, work, first, her, were, serve, swerve, hurt, shirt, purse, merge, herd, verb, jerk, clerk, bird, dirt, firm, girl, thirst, burst, church, urge, surf, purge, curve, nurse, heard, learn, search, worse, worth.*
2. And practice these 2-syllable words in the same way. *Person, early, squirrel, learn, courage, flourish, worry, surface, purchase, hurtful, courtesy.*
3. Also practice these academic and business words. *Government, international, generation, interpretation, percent, chapter, computer, consumer, transfer, perceived, perception, alternative, considerable, registered, interaction, layer, partnership, registered, parameters, error, confer, conference, emerging, undertake, internal, overall, energy.*

SOMETIMES, YOU CAN'T USE BUTTERFLY TONGUE POSITION FOR -ER-

Butterfly is the perfect position for ER *if* it occurs next to a high tense vowel like ē or a high-positioned consonant like T, D, N, L, S and SH. You can take advantage of those high positions and stay there while using the Butterfly for ER.

However, if you are saying a big, loose, round American sound like uh, ah, oh, oiy, or aow *before* the ER sound, you won't be able to use the Butterfly. Because your jaw is low and open, your tongue is too far from the top of your mouth for Butterfly. For words like that, leave your tongue in the bottom part of your mouth, tip up with the Spout, and lengthen with the Kiss. Don't worry, we are going to practice those in the next chapter.

SUMMARY

- The ER sound is usually spelled with letters ER, IR or UR, as in *her, sir, fur.* However a few important words aren't, such as *learn, courage, flourish, worry, world, worm, were*—you'll have to memorize their spellings and sounds.
- The Spout is the ER position for the tip of your tongue. Curl the tip sides inward to form a dip, creating a spout-like shape similar to the lip of a pitcher. Your ER sound will pour out this spout.
- The Kiss position helps shape your ER with your lips. Pursing your lips forward helps to extend the ER sound so it is long enough, avoiding a Russian R flick.
- The Butterfly is a high position made with the middle of your tongue. But sometimes there are low open vowels before the R, and it is not economical or easy to use the Butterfly, for example *hour, fort, car*. In those cases, just do the Spout with your tongue tip, and the Kiss with your lips.

12

▶ ▶ MORE VOWEL + R PRACTICE 🎧

THE SOUND ER is made by shaping the tongue in a certain way, and vocalizing in the throat.

This chapter is about combining vowels + ER into combinations found in words like *mark, ford, car, fear, tour, hire*. We are going to practice forming these vowel+ER sounds, gliding right from the preceding vowel to the ER connecting them into one smooth, long vowel-like sound. For the final R sound in ER, your tongue tip must not touch anywhere, which is quite different from vocalizing the vowel and flicking the R against the roof of your mouth, as one would do in Russian. Totally, totally different.

NOTE: If you've forgotten how to use the Butterfly, Spout, and Kiss positions for ER, please review the last chapter. You'll need them for the following vowel combinations.

THE ÄR GLIDE (äer)

The easiest combination is probably AH+ER in *car* and *heart*. This AH sound is usually represented by ä but sometimes by ɑ in books and dictionaries.

You won't need to do much with your lips; keep your jaw low and loose and your mouth open for AH. Glide from the ä sound into the Flute/Spout position for the ER. Curl your tongue tip slightly—just enough to make the sound while staying relaxed. Listen and imitate this manythings.org video recording of 28 words with the -ÄR- sound for your practice. Work slowly and consciously at the beginning. Keep at it until this transition from one sound to another begins to feel more comfortable and happen more quickly.

THE ĀIR GLIDE (āer)

Let's start by gliding from ā to ER. First, make the ā sound heard in the words *mate*, *say*. Then glide into the ER sound. Your tongue will be at mid-height for ā. As you move on to the ER sound, your tongue rises into the Butterfly position and its "shoulders" touch the insides of your upper molars. Maintain that soft contact and complete the ER sound using the flute and kiss movements—be sure to lengthen the combined sound (ā+ER). If you don't, you will cut off the ER sound before we have a chance to hear it.

These vowel+r glides will feel much longer than seems sensible or normal! Trust me—spend time on this sound combination, learning to lengthen it for the ER sound. Here is a practice video on Manythings.org of 29 Words with the -AIR- Sound**.**

THE ĒĒR GLIDE (ēʸer)

The ēēr sound in the word *dear* or *here* has two parts. There is the tense first part (ē) and the relaxed second part ER. Your face and mouth will change shape as you say this sound, from a wide tense lip position to the Kiss. Inside your mouth, start in the Butterfly position. Push your tongue shoulders strongly up and sideways into your upper molars. Make as much pressure as you comfortably can with your tongue's shoulders (or your butterfly's wings). Create the ē sound outside your mouth in front of your lips and let the sound slide back to your tongue 'shoulders' for the er sound as your tongue tip curls up for the final /r/. Your lips will be spread in a smile at the start, for ē, and then will relax for the ER part of the sound.

Ēēr is a long sound—it has a long duration because it takes time to make this combination of sounds and you must make it long enough to fully articulate the /r/ at the end. If you don't make the duration long enough, you will cut off that final /r/ sound—it won't have enough time to develop. Work slowly and deliberately. Use your rubber band to help you lengthen the duration of the ē and the ER.

As with the other vowel+ER sounds, keep practicing until you can glide smoothly from the vowel to the ER without losing the final R, especially if the R is not the final sound in the word. Read the words and listen to the recording. Make the ēēr sound long and tense. *Here, shear, deer, fear, clear, beer, ear, ears, earring, tears, merely, weary, leery, clearly, cheer, cheers, rear, near, nearly, peer, gear, gears, sheer, steer, steering, sneer, sneering, deer, year, bleary.*

THE ŌR GLIDE (ōer)

Let's use the word *more* as our example. First, loosen your jaw and let it hang, but keep your lips closed. Begin vibrating your vocal folds for the M, then open your mouth and make a round space for O. Keep your tongue in the bottom of your mouth. (You cannot use the Butterfly position because your mouth is open and your tongue is not high). As you end the Ō sound, flute your tongue tip and curl it up slightly for ER. Also purse your lips a bit to help lengthen the ER sound.

Practice slowly and say the sounds long enough to vibrate the final R sound in the vocal folds of your throat. Practice this video list of 33 Words with -OR.

If you say OR too briefly (which you will be tempted to do as a Russian speaker), you will cut off the final R sound before it can resonate in your vocal folds long enough for us to hear it. This won't sound natural in English. The ō + *er* combination is much longer in duration than you think.

THE ĪR GLIDE (ah+ē+er)

Fire, tire, higher, wire. These words all have an ī sound that glides into an er sound.

There are 3 sounds that blend into one: AH-ē-er.

Say AH with a big relaxed mouth opening, then raise your jaw, smile, and go to Butterfly position for *yer*.

Curl your tongue tip up, and make the Flute/Spout for the ER. Keep resonating in your vocal folds until you have fully developed the R sound at the end.

Whew! It takes a lot of changes and movement in your mouth to make this happen as one long sound. So take your time and practice slowly, gliding through *ah-yer*. Just be sure the *y* sound is a small, transitional sound connecting AH and ER.

Practice the following words and listen to the recording. The recording's URL is in the endnote of this chapter. Be sure to lengthen the sound sufficiently. *Fire, tire, retire, retirement, wire, rewire, desire, admire, expire, inspire, crier, require, liar, choir, mire, mired.*

SUMMARY

- Vowel+R are complex combinations. They are single or combination vowels that glide into the ER sound that we studied previously.
- Your mouth, jaw, and tongue positions will be different for each combination, depending on the vowel and what is required to create it. The subsequent ER will be formed with a curl of the tongue tip. Sometimes the tongue will be in the bottom of the mouth (after O and AH or AIY), but sometimes it will curl from the Butterfly position (after Ē, or Ā).
- Duration is the key to getting this right. If you say the sounds

too quickly, you'll end the sound before the final R is vocalized and your listeners won't hear it.

PART 3 CONSONANTS

Most Russian consonant sounds transfer well to English; they're quite similar. But certain consonants act like flags waving to your listeners, telling them that you are not a native speaker of English. And a few sounds (the ones with Russian flags, like V and W), tell listeners that your first language is Russian. We're going to work on consonants now.

13

WORD-INITIAL R 🎧

USING ER TO FIND R

WHEN YOU ARE comfortable making the ER sound, initial R will be much easier to pronounce.

The position of your tongue at the end of the ER sound is *exactly* the position you need for words that start with R. The following two-step process will help you make the change from Russian R to English soft initial R.

To make this easier to explain, I am going to use one word, *race*, to represent all words that start with R. We are going to use a "surgical procedure"—you will join two sounds together (ER+RA) and then "surgically" remove the front ER sound. Here's how to do it.

1. Say the ER sound and hold it for a bit. Without breaking the R sound, say ER followed by Race: *errrRace*.
2. Think about where your tongue tip is at the moment you have finished the ER part. That's the position you need to put your tongue in before you begin the word *race*. This position will give you a natural R- sound.
3. Now eliminate the actual ER sound (you can say it silently if it helps you get into position) and use the ER final tongue position when you say the word *race*.

PRACTICE

I've put together a recorded list of words with R followed by different vowels (see below). This will help you practice how to move from this new R position to other sounds.

Make sure you get into ER position with the pitcher spout (tip of tongue), the kiss (lips), and if possible, the butterfly (sides of tongue) before you start the R sound.

Reduce, rate, relegate, regulate, regulation, routine, routinely, regular, regularly, really, repeat, repeal, resume, recover, recovery, reverse, reversal, rudimentary, reliance, religion, religious, relive, relieve, relief, relocate, release, relate, relation, relationship, relative, relatively, relativity, relax, render, relent, relevant, reveal, radical, rotation, revise, revision, restful, redundant, ridiculous, rude, rook, rosary, rosemary, robot, robotic, rod, rotten, Rotterdam, reckless, rant, ripped, raw, row, repeat, redo, redone, Republican, representative, registered, registration.

Be dedicated in your practice. Even if you only have 5 minutes to spare, use them to practice so that your tongue gets used to these new habits! Persistence pays off.

SUMMARY

- The end of the ER sound is the perfect tongue position for the start of an initial R word.
- When you practice, it may help you to say a word with R in final position just before you say the word that has R at the beginning, like this *car-race.* The final R position of 'car' leaves your tongue in a good starting position for initial R in 'race'.
- If you are not able to make the ER sound yet, go back to that chapter and keep working on it until you get comfortable with

it. Then return to this chapter and do these R-initial word exercises.

14

▶ ▶ SORT OUT W AND V 🎧

A DOUBLE FLAG CHAPTER!

IN THE OLD American TV series, Star Trek, there was a Russian ensign who mixed up his V's and W's and he sounded so cute! Watch this video clip of Ensign Chekov struggling with W and V. Saying 'wery' instead of 'very' won't make you incomprehensible, but it does clearly identify you as Russian…in a cute way. But of course, 'cute' might not be what you are going for.

In English, the difference between V and W is clear and noticeable. They are two distinct sounds, made differently, and they are never confused by English speakers. But is is one of the sounds that native speaker children may take longer to master.

Russian speakers, however, often interchange V and W in English. Research hasn't clarified the reason why some people do this. As soon as I know the answer, I'll share it with you. Until then, here is an explanation of how to pronounce English V and W and a practice plan for keeping them separate.

HOW W AND V ARE DIFFERENT

V is called a 'fricative.' The word 'fricative' has the same root word as 'friction', which is what happens to your air as it passes through these small spaces and becomes turbulent. The V sound is caused by a disturbance in the airflow you produce with your upper lip and lower teeth. Gently touch the bottom of your upper teeth with your bottom lip, which narrows the space that the air can pass through and creates a vibrating sound.

HOW TO FORM V

First of all, **don't** tighten your lips into a circle. Instead, keep your lips loose and touch the bottom of your upper teeth with the edge of your lower lip. The Sounds of Speech model uses an exaggerated movement —she pulls in her bottom lip quite far below and behind the front teeth, making firm contact between the lip and the teeth. But native speakers don't usually do this, so I'm going to tell you another way that is more natural.

To create a V that is more like the one native speakers use, bring your lower lip up, and gently brush it against the edge of your upper teeth. As you say the sound, you should feel your lower lip tickle a bit as the air flow makes it vibrate against your upper teeth.

Once you can feel that you are making W and V differently, do the practice exercises below. The more times you run through these exercises, the quicker you will start to build separate muscle habits for each sound.

HOW NOT TO FORM V

Did you learn to make V like the model on the Sounds of Speech website? Go there now and watch what she is doing. This is exactly what I **don't** want you to do. She exaggerates the sound much too much! V does not have to be this forceful or exaggerated.

HOW TO FORM W

W is formed in a completely different way than V. W is a glide. Many Russian students of English learn to make W by saying ū, then schwa. If that is working for you, great! But I'm going to show you another way to make W.

W's sound is made by starting with a specific lip position, then altering the vowel sound by tightening your lips into a small open circle. W is not a consonant, although it's grouped that way for spelling. It's actually a restriction of the sound coming from your throat.

The Sounds of Speech website is helpful for W. Watch the model's mouth when she pronounces the W sound. Watch how she forms a tight circle with her lips. Imitate her. Stay relaxed as you do this. Rather than thinking of W as a consonant, think of it as a lip adjustment you make to the vowel sound you are already making (c*o*w), or to the following vowel sound if it starts the word or syllable (w*a*ter).

Your lips should be rounded into a small circle. Your jaw should be disengaged and loose. Whenever possible, your tongue should be low and relaxed, resting near or behind your lower teeth.

PRACTICE EXERCISE FOR A NATURAL W

I'm going to share a strategy with you that will help you sound more like a native speaker in English.

We are going to use the word *way* /wāē/ and do an exercise that will help you learn to make a natural W.

First, make the ā sound continuously, holding onto it until you run out of breath. Now do that again, and as you make this continuous ā sound, pull your lips together into a small circle and then quickly release them as you continue the ā sound.

Do this over and over—make the ā sound continuously as you tighten and release your lips over and over. Practice saying the ā sound smoothly and continuously as you change the sound by tightly circling and then releasing your lips. Try not to say oo or think oo as you do this. Just add a bit more energy and push the sound in your vocal folds when you make the W lip-tightening.

Now let's practice with a two-syllable word: *away* /uhwāy/. Start by making a continuous vowel sound that changes from schwa UH, to ā. Say the initial unstressed syllable's schwa, a small UH, and keep the sound going as you gradually change from ə to āāā; remember, don't break the sound. After you are able to glide continuously from ə to ā and with steady voicing, add the lips-tightening circle at the start of ā and give it more energy in your throat.

Let's do this again with the word *wet*. This time, make an ooo sound and continue it as you transition to the *-et* ending. Before you pull your lips back for *-et* (and while the sound continues) pull your lips into a small circle and release them. Once you can say ooowet comfortably, silence the oooo part and use that end position of oooo to start the word *wet*.

PRACTICE TO STRENGTHEN BOTH W AND V

Some people find they must bite (gently) on their lower lip when they make the V sound in order to make themselves conscious of the need for contact between upper teeth and lower lip. This strategy may work for you, too. But it isn't used much by native speakers of English because it slows us down when we are speaking. English isn't about perfection; it's about efficiency and fluidity. We want to make a sound that is recognizable to listeners but easy to quickly say.

1. Study the model's mouth, jaw, and lips as she says W and V on the Sounds of Speech website.
2. To find out if you are making W and V clearly and differently, speak minimal pairs of words like *wary* and *very* into a smart phone text app or into Google Translate. Does the phone or website type the correct spelling for you? Use this tool to self-evaluate your pronunciation occasionally between these exercises.

3. Practice saying Tongue Twisters with W and V: https://magoosh.com/toefl/2016/tongue-twisters-w-v/. Say them slowly and make the W *without* lip/teeth contact, and the V *with* contact. This is merely to get your muscles to begin distinguishing between the two articulations. The goal isn't to say them fast, just to say them well.
4. Practice this paragraph, pronouncing W's and V's differently, as you have learned in this chapter. *Every day we had a fun event at our school. We would race from Washington Street to Vera Way and back again. The winning team was always very happy because they went to lunch first.*
5. Find and practice W and V words here: http://manythings.org/sentences/words
6. Practice sentences with *very*, making sure you are saying V correctly here: http://www.manythings.org/sentences/words/very/1.html
7. Practice sentences with V words, such as *investigate*: http://www.manythings.org/sentences/words/investigate/1.html Remember, when you want to practice another V word, just change the final word in the URL from *investigate* to your new word choice.

If you have a persistent W/V mixup, do the above exercises often to strengthen these new muscle motor habits. You must be committed to occasional practice, or you will slip back into what is easy and unconscious—your Russian sounds.

SUMMARY

- Substituting W for V makes you sound Russian. Few other language speakers have this distinct accent challenge. It's worth working on, because it's such a distinctive marker of a Russian accent.
- W is a lip movement that alters the flow and shape of the next vowel. It's made by tightening your lips into a circle as you

begin the vowel, and doubling the length of the vowel so you have time to tighten and release your lips.
- V causes a disturbance in your air flow by gently touching your upper teeth with your lower lip as you voice the sound, letting air flow through this gentle constriction.

15

▶ ▶ MASTERING TH 🎧

THE TWO VERSIONS of English TH are different in how they are made. One of the two English TH sounds is represented by the symbol θ. It is the TH sound in words like *think, theory, tooth*. This type of TH does *not* vibrate in your throat when you say it. It's called *voiceless* or *unvoiced*. The sound is only made from causing a disturbance in the air flow; it happens just behind your teeth, using your tongue. Air flows gently out around the tongue tip and passes out between the teeth.

The other English TH sound is represented by ð. It is the TH sound in words like *that, those, weather*. This sound not only slows or stops the air flow, but it also vibrates in your throat. We call it *voiced*. It has more depth and texture and vibrates low in the throat.

The truth is, most Americans use this throaty, voiced TH as their default sound for most TH's because it's easier to join it with vowels, which are also voiced. One of the secrets to sounding like a native speaker is using whichever TH sound flows easiest in the word and phrase you are saying. So we will study both kinds of TH.

If you rest your fingertips on your vocal folds, you will feel the vibration when you say ð, but you shouldn't feel any when you make the θ sound. (This only works if you say the TH sounds in isolation; if you add a vowel sound after θ, even just the sound UH, the vowel will vibrate your vocal folds.) The other great way to recognize the difference is to put your hands over your ears when you say them. Voiced TH will be a strong, loud sound; voiceless TH will just sound like air.

For ð, the *tongue tip* is pressed against the back of the upper teeth while the vocal folds vibrate. Say 'the' and start it with your tongue pressed against the back of your teeth.

For θ, the tongue tip does not press, but sits just behind the opening between upper and lower teeth, and a rush of air flows out between the teeth and around the tongue tip. Say 'think' and let our tongue tip hover behind the gap between upper and lower teeth, touching nothing. Let air flow around your tongue and out between your teeth.

SAYING S AND Z FOR TH

If you substitute S for θ and Z for ð, here is why: You are using what feels, to you, like the closest sound in Russian. You may say '*I sink*' instead of '*I think*', and '*give me zat*' instead of '*give me that*'.

You'll have to work hard to change this articulation habit to replace S and Z, and build new TH muscle memories that are strong. Short daily workouts, practicing TH sounds at the beginning of words, middle of words, and end of words, will help your mouth and tongue become more comfortable with the new positions and remember the movements they must make.

It's just like going to a gym to work out. If you want to develop large biceps, you must do the correct exercise, and repeat it regularly. The same is true for speaking muscles. If you want to be able to use TH sounds, you must practice the sounds regularly.

Here's another metaphor: learning new sounds is also like learning to play a musical instrument, or doing a new sports movement, or a new dance step. There are certain movements that must become automatic. You must be able to do them without thinking about them. Speaking, and pronunciation, is like that. You can't stop and think about where to put your tongue for TH, it must happen naturally as you speak. You must develop durable muscle memories and habits, and the only way to do that is to work them out as if you're going to the gym, frequently, in short sessions.

YOUR 'TH' PRACTICE PLAN

Follow the same 4 steps that you used for vowels earlier.

1. Raise your awareness with listening practice at Manythings.org/pp with lessons #6 and #10

2. Compare how these sounds are made. Go to http://soundsofspeech.uiowa.edu Compare how the model says S and Z, and how she says the 2 TH sounds, θ, ð. Study her jaw, her lips, and her tongue if you can see it.

3. Strengthen your control with minimal word pairs of sounds using English Club online. Here are some practice lists:

S vs. θ words https://www.englishclub.com/pronunciation/minimal-pairs-s-th.htm

Z vs. TH words https://www.englishclub.com/pronunciation/minimal-pairs-th-z.htm

4. Strengthen your TH sounds in context by practicing them in words and sentences you find in your searches at http://manythings.org/sentences/words

SENTENCES WITH TH WORDS

Following are links to sentences with frequently used TH words, on Manythings.org. It's the same link, over and over, changing only the word you want to study. Pick one of these links below and go through as many sentences as you can in 10 minutes. Then take a break and return to it again later today or tomorrow. Keep building and strengthening your speech muscle habits and memories.

Both TH sounds, θ and ð (voiced and voiceless) are included in different positions (initial, final, middle).

VOICED TH WORDS

If you're reading this in e-book format, the links will take you straight there. If you're reading this in paperback, follow along on the website page provided to you, or use this link: http://www.manythings.org/sentences/words/the/ for all the words. Just change the end word to the next one (i.e. change /the/ to /they/.

The

They

That

This

There

VOICELESS, AIRY TH WORDS

Thursday

Through

Think

WORD FINAL TH

South

Truth

Worth

Health

MIDDLE OF THE WORD TH

Something

Nothing

Method

Father

Mother

SUMMARY

- S and TH (θ) have similarities and differences, but it's the differences you must focus on: relax your tongue tip for θ, position it behind your teeth, lightly touching them and let the air flow out alongside your tongue.
- Z and TH (ð) have similarities but you must focus on the differences: for Z, your tongue tip is held back away from your teeth and it doesn't touch them; for TH, the tongue tip gently presses against the back of your upper teeth and the sound is made in your throat.
- Substituting S and Z for TH is a very telling accent marker for Russian speakers of English.

16

T, D, L, AND N

SMALL TWEAKS HERE WILL SMOOTH OUT YOUR ENGLISH SOUND

IN RUSSIAN, there is more *horizontal* movement of your tongue for these 4 sounds, while in English, there is more *vertical* movement from a lower jaw position. All 4 Russian sounds are dental sounds, made by the tongue tip pressing against the back of your upper teeth. But the 4 English sounds are alveolar—they are made by touching the tongue tip to different locations and ways, to the alveolar bumps on the roof of your mouth.

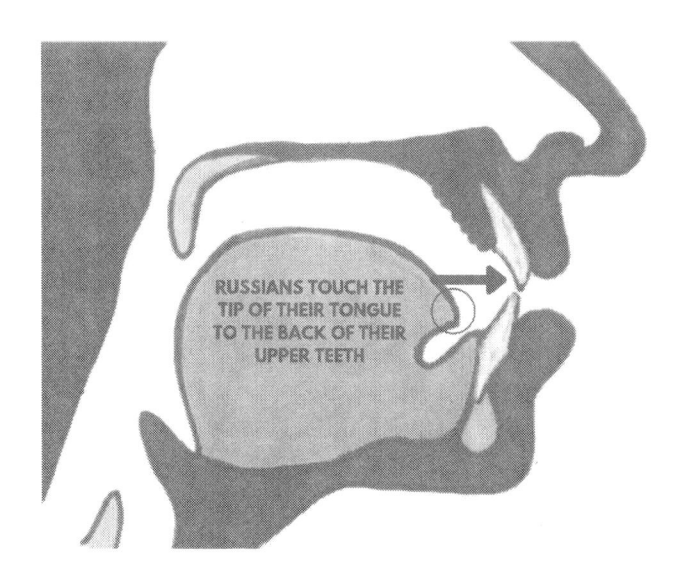

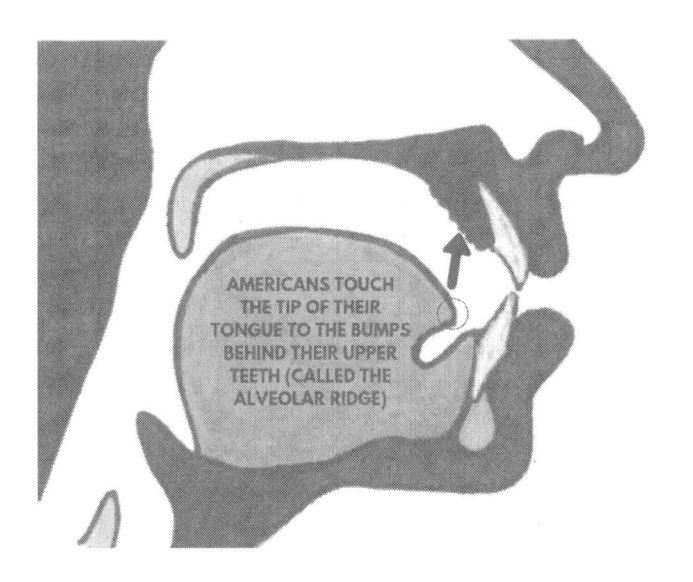

AMERICANS TOUCH THE TIP OF THEIR TONGUE TO THE BUMPS BEHIND THEIR UPPER TEETH (CALLED THE ALVEOLAR RIDGE)

For these English sounds, work on tightening your tongue tip and touching or pressing it against the alveolar bumps.

American T is made with a tense tongue tip that touches just behind the place where upper teeth meet the first alveolar bumps. In American English, it is voiceless in stressed position, and voiced in unstressed syllables.

American D is made in the same area, but with a softer tongue tip gently pressing against the alveolar bumps just a bit further back than T. It is voiced, so it is throatier than T.

American L is often made a tiny bit further back than D, using a soft tongue tip and very little pressure. Gently touch the alveolar bumps with your tongue for L.

American N is made by broadly pressing the front of the tongue against the alveolar bumps, using a much wider surface area of the tongue.

HOW TO HOLD YOUR JAW

The difference between the Russian sounds and the American English sounds is tied to the position and tension of your lower jaw, which allows for the position of your tongue tip.

In Russian, the lower jaw is held higher, which allows for a smaller oral cavity, and that leads to more forward and backward movement of the tongue in this narrow space.

In English, though, the lower jaw is held more loosely and lower, which means that the tongue is also in a lower position and so it must reach up higher to touch the alveolar bumps on the roof of the mouth.

Here's a way to feel the difference: say the name 'Natasha' as you normally would in Russian. With your jaws this close together, up and down movements of the tongue are difficult to make, so the Russian tongue moves forward and presses against the back of the upper teeth for the T.

Listen to how Natasha is spoken by the movie clip on Playphrase.me. Type in the word NATASHA. You'll see 3 clips. The man's voice is the most "American" pronunciation. You can hear that he drops his jaw and makes much bigger AH sounds.

But here's how American's say it. First, relax your jaw and let it hang *loose* and *low*. With your jaw low like this, raise just your tongue tip to touch the alveolar bumps on the roof of your mouth just behind your upper teeth for N. This lower jaw position makes a much larger opening and a bigger space for the vowels to be formed in. Now the tongue can go vertical and make a bigger, explosive movement with lots of air around it for the T. With your jaw lower, your mouth will be more open, which makes the second A in Natasha, the ä/ah sound, a bigger, more forward sound that floats out of your mouth. No sounds are swallowed; everything is released and released forward.

This difference creates a slight but noticeable accent. It's the difference between a closed and open oral cavity. It doesn't affect your comprehensibility, but does act like a mini-flag that tells your listeners you are probably Russian.

SUMMARY

- T is made with a tight tongue tip that touches the alveolar bumps behind your upper teeth.
- D is made with a softer tongue tip that presses against the first alveolar bumps, and your tongue may also touch the top of your upper teeth because the tip doesn't have to be as tight as for T.
- L is made with a soft tongue tip that presses gently against the middle alveolar bumps.
- N is made with a softer tongue tip, pressing gently and broadly against most of the alveolar bumps.
- English often requires an oral cavity like a cave, big and open. Hold your jaw low and loose while you practice reaching up with your tongue tip to touch against your alveolar bumps.

17

🎧 CLEAR L & DARK L 🎧

A SPLIT PERSONALITY

LIKE W AND V, how you pronounce L can tell your listeners about your first language. As a Russian speaker, you know very well how to make a strong, "dark" L sound in the back of the mouth; your tongue squeezes and reaches up in the back. English has a similar dark L, a back-positioned sound which is a smaller, weaker version of your Russian L. English speakers use the dark L when L is in final position, at the end of words.

But English has another kind of L, that you may not have learned in your English classes. It's called a "clear" L. It is articulated in the front of the mouth with a tightened tongue tip that pushes off quickly and firmly from the alveolar bumps just behind your upper teeth. It has a lighter, more forward sound than the dark L. It's use at the start of words and stressed syllables.

COMPARING OUR DARK Ls

For Russian dark L, the back of the tongue raises up and presses backward energetically toward the back of the throat, restricting the space that the air must flow through.

For English dark L, the jaw is low and relaxed and the tongue rests low, which keeps the oral cavity more open and wider for a greater air flow. The biggest difference is the amount of tension in the tongue backward movement—the English dark L articulation is more relaxed than the Russian one.

MORE ABOUT THE AMERICAN L SOUNDS

There are 3 ways English native speakers may produce an L sound.

The English clear L is made by touching the tongue tip to the alveolar bumps behind the upper teeth, leaving the back of the tongue relaxed. The English dark L is made by relaxing the front of the tongue, but moving the back of the tongue up toward the velum, or soft palate, narrowing the space that air and sounds pass through.

Sometimes native English speakers even use both front and back movements together (see the third image). Don't worry about trying this right now. Eventually, when you are truly comfortable using the front and back positions for L, you will do what native speakers do—use whichever tongue position is easiest in that moment of speaking.

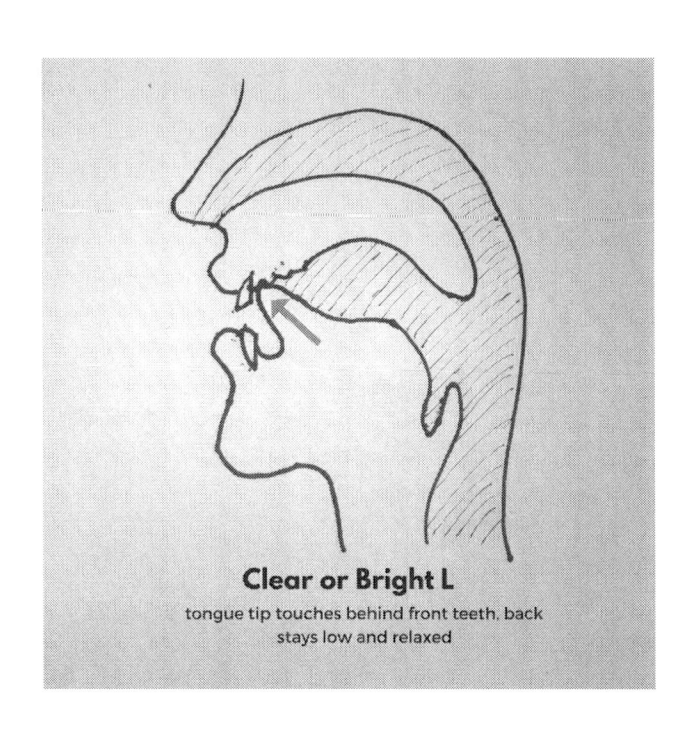

Clear or Bright L
tongue tip touches behind front teeth, back stays low and relaxed

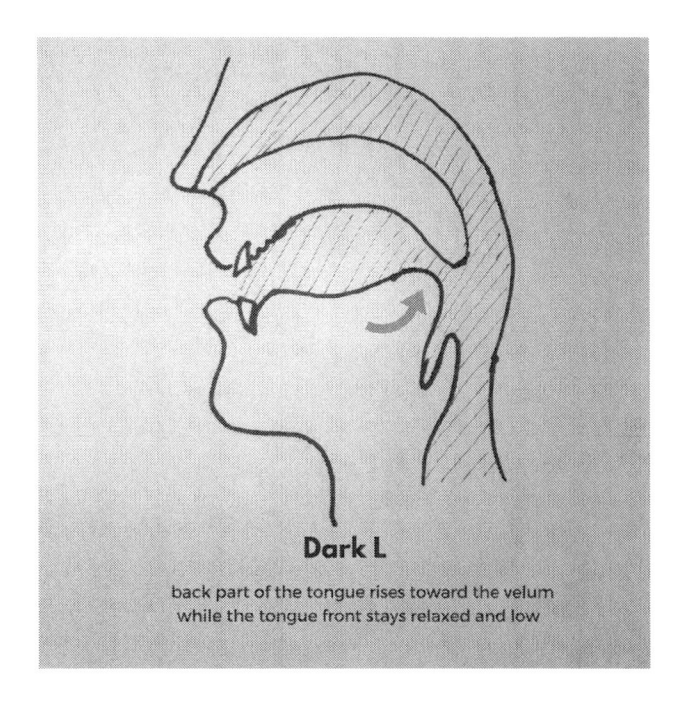

Dark L
back part of the tongue rises toward the velum while the tongue front stays relaxed and low

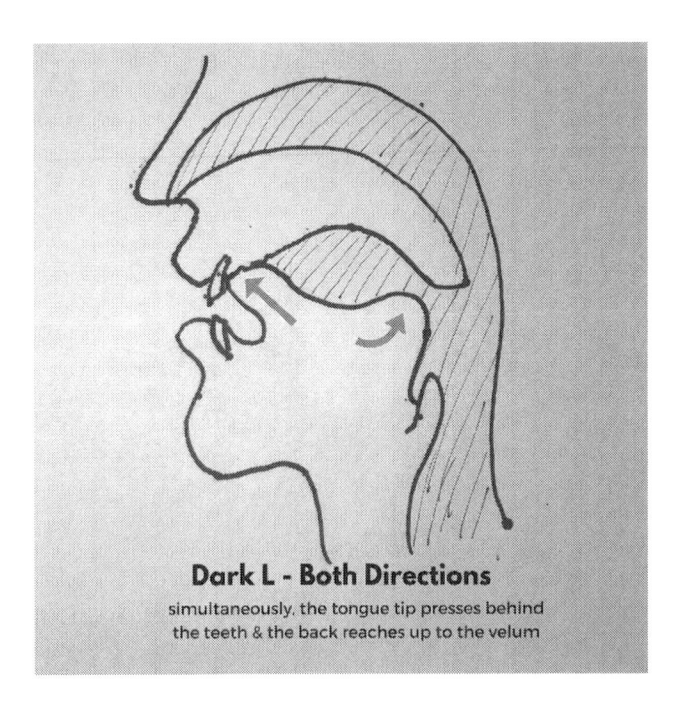

Dark L - Both Directions
simultaneously, the tongue tip presses behind
the teeth & the back reaches up to the velum

CLEAR L

English's clear, forward L is completely different from both Russian and English dark Ls. Raise your tongue tip up, and press it either against the alveolar bumps behind the upper teeth, or press it where your upper teeth meet the roof of your mouth. The sides of the tongue may pull inward gently to allow air to pass around it. Release the tip while making the L sound in your throat and let it dissolve into the following vowel. Often English learners make the L too short or clipped, or they push too hard with their tongue tip. Let clear L blend into the following vowel as one long, changing sound. Both L and vowels are *voiced*—they both vibrate the vocal folds, so they blend together easily.

Remember—Your tongue tip touches the roof of your mouth near the top of your upper teeth, and the sides of your tongue are pulled in, the back of your tongue is low and relaxed, and your jaw is loose. Release your tongue tip as you make the vowel sound following the L. Don't worry about air flow. It will move gently over and around your tongue as you pronounce the L and the next vowel.

Use Sounds of Speech to check that you can make the clear L as the model does. Notice her relaxed, loose jaw and lips.

Clear Ls either start a word or start a syllable. If the L begins a stressed syllable that is in the middle of a word, like *align* or *alone*, your jaw position will be low because of the previous schwa sound. Keep your jaw relaxed and low, and let your tongue do the moving. If L is in the middle of a word and begins an unstressed syllable, as in the word *syllable*, it can be made with less pressure and more softly than if it's starting out the word or signaling a stressed syllable.

The following clear and dark L word lists are combined onto one recording. Pause the recording as you read and move from list to list.

PRACTICE CLEAR L

For clear Ls, connect your tongue tip to the flesh above your upper teeth, and then blend into the following vowel.

INITIAL L— lecture, load, lace, light, like, lit, lock, late, load, loose, lark, land, law, luck, later.

MIDDLE L— align, relative, relax, slowly, carefully, softly, elevate, alone, follow, below, allow, elite, online, unlikely

Pause the recording now, until you are ready to continue with the dark L words that follow.

DARK L

For English dark L, it's the opposite. Like the Russian L sound, the back of your tongue squeezes at the base and raises, while the front part of your tongue rests behind your lower teeth. **But don't reach as far back, don't squeeze as hard, and don't go up as high in the**

back, as you do for Russian L. This movement is smaller and more relaxed than Russian L.

PRACTICE WORDS FOR DARK L

This recording is part of the above link.

final, verbal, real

fold, hold, mold, told

file, trial, dial, fuel

foal, fail, mail, goal

curl, furl, twirl, world, girl

* * *

Practice the following word lists slowly, consciously and carefully. Remember to connect your tongue tip for initial positions, and ease up a little for final positions.

BOTH Ls IN ONE PHRASE

When a word ends in dark L, and the next word begins with clear L, you can link the L's together and use the easier clear L movement for both Ls: final + lesson = finaLLesson. These are on the same recording as the above lists.

the final lesson (dark L in final, clear L in lesson)

goal loss (dark L in goal, clear L in loss)

a whole lot (dark L in whole, clear L in lot)

CLEAR L BEFORE DARK L

Practice switching from the clear, tongue-tip L to the back-squeeze dark L. Included on the above recording.

less coal (clear, tongue-tip L in *less*, dark, back L in *coal*)

a light file (clear L in *light*, dark L in *file*)

a little cold (clear L in *leave*, dark L in *cold*)

a long tail (clear L in *long*, dark L in *tail*)

lay still (clear L in *lay*, dark L in *still*)

SUMMARY

- English dark L is more relaxed than Russian L. It is made by pressing the back of your tongue diagonally up toward the velum in the back of your mouth, but not as far back, and not as far up.
- English clear L is created with the tip of the tongue touching or pressing against the alveolar bumps. The rest of the tongue can be relaxed. This is a forward sound.
- L is often pronounced too quickly. Let L blend into the vowel; this will help extend the duration of your vowels.

18

ENGLISH H

CLEAN YOUR EYEGLASSES FOR A PERFECT H!

TO MAKE the sound of English H, pretend to clean your eyeglasses. Release a puff of air out through a relaxed open throat and mouth.

English H is not really like Russian letter x, but that is often how it is pronounced by Russians.

THE DIFFERENCE BETWEEN H AND RUSSIAN X

For Russian x, your tongue moves backward toward the soft tissue at the back of the mouth to create a narrow passageway for the air flow, which causes a great deal of turbulence. The sound and turbulence begin at the back of the mouth and it is sharp and strong.

English H is made quite differently. Keep your tongue lying flat in the bottom of your mouth. This creates an open space for the air coming up from your lungs to move forward in your mouth without restriction.

Go to Sounds of Speech and watch the interactive demonstration of the H sound. Pay attention to the tongue movement, then think about what your tongue does when you pronounce the Russian letter 'x' and compare the two sounds. Russian X narrows the space that the air must pass through; while English H position is really just a widening of the mouth with an exhalation as people do when they blow air on their eyeglasses before cleaning them.

PRACTICE: *Clean your glasses at the start of 'it' to form the word 'hit'. Blend the H air into the I vowel for a continuous sound.*

Be sure to relax and lower your jaw, keep your tongue low, and exhale air as if you are cleaning your eyeglasses and you want as much air to exit as possible.

When English H comes in the middle of a word, do this same action and go right into the following vowel—the H-exhalation and the vowel become one sound.

The following words have different vowels following the H exhalation so you can practice with different vowel positions.

Both H-word lists, initial H and middle H, are on this recording.

'H' AT THE START OF A WORD

Open your mouth and exhale as you continue the word:

happy, hit, heat, hay, him, who, how, hook, hope, hot, hawk, hurl, hug, heavy, high

'H' IN THE MIDDLE

In the middle of a word, the H sound at the beginning of a stressed syllable is made the same way, but it can be smaller:

inherit, adhere, inhabit, behave, comprehend, mahogany, behind, sea hawk, yahoo, megahertz, dehumidifier, alcohol

SUMMARY

- Pretend you are cleaning your eyeglasses; relax your jaw,

relax and lower your tongue, and exhale a puff of air. That's English H.
- English H and Russian letter 'x' are not the same sound.
- Keep your tongue relaxed and flat for English H. Don't let it move backward toward the soft palate and don't let it move upward; both movements restrict the flow of air. You want to let that air flow freely and fully.

19

P, T, AND K SOUNDS

NEVER FEAR SPITTING ON YOUR FRIENDS AGAIN

AS A RUSSIAN SPEAKER, you don't have any problems with voiced sounds like B, G, and D. But when it comes to their twin unvoiced sounds, P, K and T, you may have difficulty finding just the right pronunciation. Since P, K, and T are not aspirated in Russian, they may sound more like B, G, and D. Listeners might hear *bit* when you meant to say *pit*, *bag* when you meant *back*, and *hid* instead of *hit*.

Study the sounds under the two tabs, *voiceless* and *voiced*, on Sounds of Speech. Listen for the voiced throat vibrations of B, G, and D. Listen for the lack of throat vibrations in P, K, and T.

Put your hand on your throat when you say B and feel the vibration. Leave your hand there and say P—only the P sound, not pu, pa, pi. If you only make the P sound, you won't feel any vibration; that may come from any vowel sound you put after it.

An even stronger way to feel the difference between B and P, T and D, and K and G, is to put your hands over your ears and say B, then P. B will echo in your head. P, pronounced by itself (no vowel sound), will not echo.

As you experiment with P, K, and T, you may over-compensate by putting *too* much air and energy into them. My students sometimes ask, jokingly, how to make the sounds correctly without spitting on their conversation partners.

If you're wondering this also, here is the what to do so you can avoid such an embarrassing situation.

THE CURE

First of all, stop thinking about these sounds as compression bombs (I don't mean digital viruses, I mean exploding soda bottles). Please don't tightly compress your lips and then follow with an explosion! Instead, think about P, K, and T as gentle movements that briefly stop the flow of air.

For P, you should put your lips together gently. Don't squeeze or press your lips together tightly. Don't push the P sound out. Hold your lips together lightly to stop the airflow, then release the air built up behind them, and let the vowel sound flow out. If you think of P as a gentle stop-and-release movement, rather than as an explosion, you won't be spitting on your friends!

K's job, also, is to momentarily and gently break up the flow of air, using the top-back of the tongue. Like P, try to use the least amount of pressure and the smoothest possible air flow.

Guess what I'm going to say for T? Yep! T's job is to momentarily and gently break up the flow of air, using a tightened tongue tip. Make contact somewhere in the area of the alveolar bumps.

The basic rule is to relax your compression and use a soft, full flow of air, and there will be no chance of you spitting on your friends.

P, T, AND K CHANGE SLIGHTLY IN UNSTRESSED SYLLABLES

There's something else that's important for you to learn. Each of these sounds, P, T and K, can change from a stronger, airier sound to a smaller, more muted sound, depending on its position in a word.

P, K, T are given the most air and have no throat vibrations when they start a word or a stressed syllable. But if they occur as unstressed or at the end of a word, they lose their power and air flow. Watch my YouTube video about how and why Americans reduce consonant sounds when they speak.

But remember, these three sounds need to be completely unvoiced when they begin a word or a stressed syllable.

This is a common feature of English stress. It's important for your listener to clearly catch sounds at the beginning of spoken words so they can anticipate what you are saying. This is true for stressed syllables also, which are very important for listeners to hear.

However, in *unstressed* syllables, it would be misleading if these sounds were strongly pronounced, so native speakers relax and reduce them. In unstressed positions, P can almost sound like a soft B. T may sound more like a soft D. And K might sound more like a soft G. How a sound is pronounced is always dependent on its position in the word.

PRACTICE

Study P, K, and T on Sounds of Speech.

Use minimal pairs of words, like **bin** and **pin**, to help you learn to make these unvoiced sounds more naturally.

There is no shortage of minimal pair word lists on the internet. Type **minimal pairs B and P** into your search bar, and up will pop lists of words with voiced B and unvoiced P to practice. Do the same for G and K. And again for T and D.

Be sure to include practice words which have P, K, or T followed by tense vowels (ā, ē, and ī) such as *Pete, parent, pie, cake, Keith, kite, take, tea, type*. These are the combinations that can result in too much spray.

SUMMARY

- Initial P and stressed syllable P are formed with lips gently touching, but not pressed together or squeezed tightly. Just break the flow of air, and then open your lips and allow the backed-up air to flow out with the next sound.
- Initial T and stressed syllable T are formed by gently touching the alveolar bumps, behind your upper teeth. Don't press tightly, don't explode the sound, simply break the air flow and then let it flow around your tongue and out of your mouth as you finish the word.
- Initial K, and stressed syllable K is formed the same way, using a different tongue part. Gently and momentarily break the air flow by gently pressing the top of your tongue, halfway back, against the roof of your mouth momentarily. Let the airflow resume to finish the word.

PART 4 INTONATION AND PITCH

Of all the things in this book that you will work on, these in Part 4 may be the most important to get right.

There are some basic changes you must make to communicate fully and more like a native speaker. This section is about pitch, intonation, and the sound variations that are used for phrase and sentence stress in English. Here are the 5 changes we will work on.

1. Change your **pitch** use. English uses more of the musical notes in its range. Russian uses low and high notes.
2. Highlight (stressing) **important words** in new ways. English has more and different stress requirements than Russian.
3. Change your question intonation **patterns** so you don't confuse listeners.
4. Learn how to **exclaim** and express surprise or consternation in English.
5. Signal to your listeners about the start of a **new topic** or change in conversation.

We are all born able to recognize our first language pitch and intonation use—we learn it when we are in the womb. This means you may very well be using Russian tone and pitch patterns in English without realizing it.

While this won't make it difficult for native speakers to understand your words, it can easily cause a misunderstanding or breakdown in communication as your English listeners become confused about your meaning, attitude, and intentions.

You wouldn't want to be saying all the right things yet still leave a negative impression, so study the chapters in Part 4 well.

20

WORD STRESS IN SENTENCES 🎧

WE STRESS IMPORTANT WORDS, BUT WE DO IT DIFFERENTLY

WHEN I LISTEN to the intonation of Russian, I hear a steady low intonation, with sudden spikes and drops in pitch to signal accentuated information.

When I listen to the intonation of English, I hear frequent pitch movement and changes, with graded tone movement going up for accentuated information, and sloping down again on following words. It's much more gradual, and constantly moving up and down.

Newly spoken nouns, verbs, adjectives, and adverbs are especially critical for your listener to hear so they sit at the top of English intonation curves. These words are the core of your spoken message. The rest of the words have supporting roles, grammatically and syntactically, and can be lowered in tone or dropped into an intonation valley where they are less attention-seeking to your listener.

For example, in the phrase '*of the doctor*', the 2 vowels in *of* and *the* are reduced to very short, very weak sounds. It becomes əvðə. All the sounds are reduced to the least possible state that can still be recognized by listeners. This creates an audible contrast between the focus word, *doctor*, and the supporting low-value words, *of* and *the*.

We are going to study how to highlight the most important parts of your message. Here is the link to a recording of **all** the practice sentences in this chapter—you can listen as you read, pausing when necessary. After you finish reading this chapter, listen to the recording again and identify which words I stressed most. Think about why I stressed them and how I stressed them, and mimic my strategies.

NEW INFORMATION WORD STRESS

As a general rule, we not only put new information on top of these intonation curves, but we also say the word a bit longer, clearer, stronger.

We will use a system of *italicized* and **bolded** words in our practice, to help you practice this.

Italicized words will be the *important information* of your message. Don't forget that multi-syllable words each have their own stressed syllable that is longer, stronger, and possibly higher in pitch than the other syllables in that word.

Bolded words are your **key** words — the one word that drives your whole sentence. It has the most prominent place in the sentence—it represents your theme. Give it more stress, a higher pitch, a longer duration than the other words in the sentence

He *went* to the **store**.

I *called* her **last** night. OR I **called** her last night.

Let's *stop* and see **James** on our way.

   I for*got* to tell you…I *paid* the **rent** yesterday.

STRESS IN COMPLEX SENTENCES

As you can see from the examples above, when your sentences get longer and more complex, you may have more than one important word you want to highlight.

Give the greatest stress to the word that is your reason for speaking—that's your **key word**. Don't go as high in pitch as you would in Russian. Keep your tone undulating over hills and valleys of sound in your mid-range. Let your *important words* slide over the hilltops. Put your key word on the top of its own intonation curve. Your other important words should be in your middle range, higher than the low tone function words, but lower than your key words.

Conversation examples:

> A. I *walked* the *dog*.
> B. **What** *dog*???
> A. The *neighbors* got a **dog** and *hired* me to **walk** it.
> B. What **breed** is it?
> A. I have *no clue*, but it's **cute**!

* * *

> A. When you *get* to the **light**, *turn* **right**.
> B. I thought it was a **left** turn.
> A. If you turn **left**, you'll come to a *dead-end*.
> B. *Good* to *know*.

SHOW WHAT MATTERS MOST

The above aren't *rules*, they're *patterns* that native speakers use because they work. We all use this system and our children learn it automatically. But you can override these patterns whenever you need to put special stress on something. Use *longer* duration, *higher* pitch, and *stronger* articulation to send a clear message or give special emphasis to something in your message.

You *may* choose to highlight a pronoun or preposition if that helps you *clarify* your message. Remember, the goal is to communicate with someone **quickly** and **efficiently**.

EXAMPLES

Actually, I asked you to put it **on** the table, *not* **under** it. Would you **move** it **please**?

* * *

A. Is *this* **your** *binder*?
B. No, *mine* has a **blue sticker** on the back. It *might* be **Brad's**.
A. *No*, **his** is *different* from this.

PRACTICE: FOCUS FOR YOUR LISTENERS

Our goal in the next section is for you to practice alternating your stress if you have two words you want to highlight.

Quick reminder: don't spike up and drop down quickly as you would in Russian. Make intonation curves that smoothly rise for key words, and gradually fall on supporting phrases.

Each of the following 12 sentences has two important words in the message. When a spoken phrase or sentence has two focus words they both are emphasized, but differently. Remember, you must lengthen the vowel, and you can accentuate it more with energy, clarity, higher pitch, or a combination.

In the practice sentences below, say the **bolded** focus word slightly higher and more strongly than the *italicized* focus word. Let all the other words shrink and relax.

Whenever you use an intonation curve to draw attention to a key word, let your tone change move smoothly up to the key word, then gently down to middle or lower range for supporting words.

Don't move sharply up and down as Russian does. Learn to glide and slide in waves of sound.

In the following pairs of sentences, change which word gets the higher pitch and which gets the lower pitch.

I'm **very** happy to *meet* you.

I'm *very* happy to **meet** you.

She *said* she was taking a **taxi**.
She **said** she was taking a *taxi*.

They're so *sorry* to see you **go**.
They're so **sorry** to see you *go*.

I'll **call** you when I *get* there.
I'll *call* you when I **get** there.

I *wonder* what he's **doing** here.
I **wonder** what he's *doing* here.

I'm *ready* when **you** are.
I'm **ready** when *you* are.

She wore a **beautiful** *red* dress.
She wore a *beautiful* **red** dress.

There are **too** many *people* here.
There are *too* many **people** here.

The closest **store** is a *mile* away.
The closest *store* is a **mile** away.

Lock the *door* when you leave.
Lock the **door** when you leave.

Thank you for calling me *back*.
Thank you for calling me **back**.

PRACTICE: PLAYPHRASE.ME

Go to PlayPhrase.me and make sure that it is set for English, then type in a common phrase like "Who are you talking to?" You'll hear many clips from movies and TV shows of actors saying those same words. The actor's tone and intonation will vary greatly depending on the situation, need, and mood.

Mimic these actors using the same intonation pattern and speed that they do. Pay close attention to which words get more stress and which words get less. Squeeze the less important words together and slow down on the important words.

This is a great exercise to help you speak faster and sound more native-like and it's a lot of fun to do with friends. Get silly and mimic the tonal movement that you hear. Ask your study buddy to tell you when your tone moves like the actor's tone.

Don't worry about the context or what is happening in the scene between the actors. Just practice modulating your voice to duplicate the variety of tones used by these actors for this one phrase. Stretch your vowels if they do. Swallow them if they do. Think of it as singing exercises—you are learning to use your speaking voice in a different way than you are accustomed to doing.

Practice a new phrase every week, and go over all the variations during the week. Eventually they'll get easier to say and will come more quickly. You'll get used to using a wider range of tones in a more natural manner.

PRACTICE: NUANCE

Now that we've talked about the basics of word stress, let's explore how native speakers use different kinds of stress to add more richness, more continuity, more nuance or implied meaning into the conversation. These are the messages you may be missing, and you possibly aren't sending. They help immensely in conversations, even in speeches.

Go to Playphrase.me and type in this phrase:

could do that

Listen carefully to each video clip, over and over, until you can hear which of these 3 words, *could, do,* or *that*, gets the most stress in each example. Hypothesize why that particular word got the most stress in that conversation. Do this now before you read on.

* * *

Ok, you've listened to the clips! Did you notice that…

Some of the actors stress the word DO, as in the example where the actor says: "Do you think you could **do** *that for me?*", the speaker is asking if the listener is *willing* to do it. In the example "Good thieves could **do** that", the speaker is stating that thieves have the *ability* to do it.

Some of the actors stress the word COULD. In the example "Yeah, I **could** do that, but I…", the speaker is stressing the possibility of him doing something, however his long stretch on the word *could,* and the use of a higher pitch, and the non-finality of the middle pitch on 'that' (rather than a final low pitch) foreshadows the "but" that follows.

Some actors give the word THAT the highest stress in the phrase. In "I could do **that**", Can you hear their voices glide upward in pitch on 'that'? In the example, "Only a mother could cause **that** much damage", his voice leaps up in pitch on 'that' as an expression of something extreme. In these, the speakers are pointing with their pitch to something that is already known between them.

PRACTICE: IMMERSION

Imagine *yourself* saying "I **could** do that, but…" and meaning that it would be possible for you to do that thing. Stretch out your tone on the word *could* as the actor does, and bend the vowel a bit to signal that you are not firm in your commitment to the idea.

Imagine yourself saying "I could do **that**!", giving *that* more height and energy than *could*. Imagine that you are reassuring your friend that you can do this favor for them .

Imagine yourself saying "I could **do** that" implying that you are capable and willing to do something.

The pitch levels used for the focus word and for the drop afterwards are never as high or as low, and never as sharp, as they are in Russian. Make gentle, mid-range intonation hillsides that glide smoothly up and drop gently down after the focus word.

Use Playphrase.me or any video you like, and study tone use and accentuation. Which words get the very most stress? What kind of stress is it—is it a raised pitch? Is it merely a longer duration? Does it have more energy? Is it a combination? Analyze what is happening and observe why it's happening, then imitate them as you consider the speaker's state of mind and situation.

SUMMARY

- Important words receive more stress, which means giving the stressed syllable a longer duration, more strength, and possibly a higher pitch (but not a Russian high spike in pitch).
- Unimportant words receive less stress, meaning they are softer, shorter, and less articulated.
- The last important word in a sentence often gets even more stress than all the others.
- Native speakers modulate their duration, energy, and pitch to stress the truly important words in their message—these are words that maintain the threads of the conversation, introduce new ideas, emphasize a point the speaker wants to make, or add nuance and innuendo.

21

▶ ▶ INTONATION IS CRITICAL 🎧

IT'S NOT WHAT YOU SAY BUT HOW YOU SAY IT

LET'S talk about tone and intonation. When I say *tone*, I'm talking about the changes you make in the pitch placement of each syllable and the resulting impression you give to listeners. Changes in your tones can affect how people perceive you.

Intonation is a string of tones in a pattern that your listeners will rely on to interpret your message. As listeners, we 'follow you forward'. Hearing the start of an expected intonation pattern allows us to listen forward to your idea, rather than focusing on each word.

Tone is a big deal to native English speakers—it's very important. Stress patterns and tonal miscues are harder for native English speakers to process than simple mispronunciations or grammar mistakes. Using the right intonation pattern can make you sound engaging and approachable, like someone a native speaker can converse with. The wrong patterns can make you sound rude, bored, or sullen.

Questions are good examples of 'tone gone wrong'. Russian question intonation patterns begin with a high pitch placement at the start and then quickly and steadily move downward in pitch until the end. Unfortunately, this specific tonal pattern, in English, expresses *negativity or disapproval*, rather than an engaging question.

COMPARING OUR QUESTION CONTOURS

Below are two graphs generously shared by Christiane Fleur Crosby [1], comparing the different intonation patterns used by Russian and English speakers when they say the same question in their own language.

The *dotted* lines are Russian. The *solid* lines are English. The top graph compares Russian information questions and English Wh-question patterns (who, what, when, where, why, how). The bottom graph shows yes/no question patterns. See how the peaks of sound are different in their location and height?

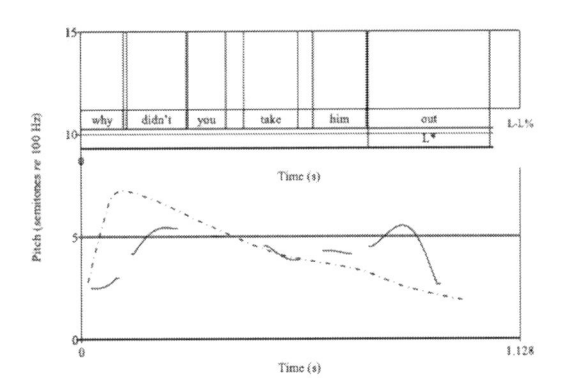

Figure 9. Russian information question contour (dotted line) superimposed on an English *wh*-question contour for comparison.

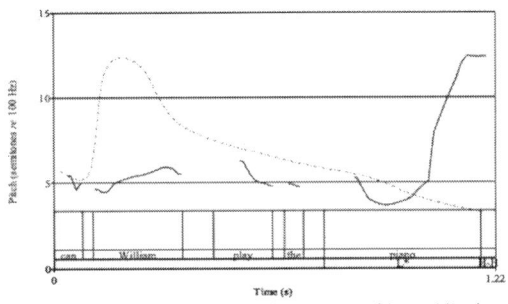

Figure 10. Russian *yes-no* question contour (dotted line) superimposed on an English *yes-no* question contour for comparison.

Both Russian Wh- questions and yes/no questions start high and end low. However in English, Wh- questions rise in tone on the Wh- word and rise again on the noun or verb that is being asked about. English yes/no questions have a mid-to-low tone modulation, but end high on the noun or verb being asked about.

If you are using Russian question contours and pitch movement when you ask a question in English, you are conveying a different attitude toward your listener than you think. The sharp rise followed by a quick drop, which is normal in Russian, is confusing, at best, and at worst, sounds harsh or demanding. This pattern—a high rise in pitch followed by a quick drop—is not neutral or inviting in English. It is used for negative expressions.

To give the right impression—to communicate your friendly intentions—you must understand how to use English patterns of intonation. The more aware of them you are, the better you will get at this. You *will* get better if you keep paying attention to the patterns native speakers use, and mimicking them.

PRACTICE FOR WH-QUESTIONS

1. This is such a fun way to study intonation. It will help you think about the changes you must make in your English intonation. Go to playphrase.me and type in the question: **Where are you going?** You'll hear many variations spoken by different actors. Some actors sound upset, some relaxed, but all use the same intonational movement: it begins just below or at mid-pitch on the first word *where*, then drops down in the middle with a little stress for focus words, and finishes on a higher pitch on the stressed syllable of the important verb, *going*. There is only one exception in this group of examples, the Harry Potter actor. In this example, the boy is using a downward tone movement in his intonation because he is bullying someone. He pitches downward as he says 'going' instead of rising on the pitch, to sound more threatening. None

of the other actors push down on *going* because they want to engage in conversation with the listener. Tone movement is usually unconscious and often not noticed by English students when they listen to native speakers. But it's so very important. Listen to all the movie clips, think about their tone movement and the situation of the speakers, and imitate them, imagining you are in the same situation.

2. Next, I want you to say 'Where are you going?' in Russian and think about the intonation contour that is natural for you to use. Compare that contour to the English contours you heard on playphrase.me. Do you hear what you must do differently? Practice asking common questions using English intonation contours. Then say the same questions in Russian. Go back to English again. You must be able to move back and forth in tone patterns between Russian and English so you can develop two sets of intonation patterns and use them when you need them.

3. Do this exercise again on playphrase.me using simple Wh-question phrases or sentences (who, what, when, where, why, how). Pay close attention to the intonation patterns actors use for each Wh-word, and listen also for which other word is emphasized. No matter what the stressed words of the question are, a Wh-question follows the same pattern of *higher ending on a final peak followed by a drop.*

4. Now do this whole process again, this time with common Yes-No questions such as: **Are you happy?** Repeat the process: listen to all the examples, listen for the common contour, and compare that to your familiar contour for the same question in Russian. Remember, Yes/No intonation contours are different than Wh- questions; they go continuously up at the end.

5. Now broaden your studies. Listen to your favorite TV actor's intonations. When he/she says something that 'catches your ear', repeat that phrase or sentence and draw a line for the intonation contour that you hear the speaker use. (Start with a short sentence!) Next, write the actual spoken words where they land on that contour line, and notice which words are on

the tops of the contour, (higher in pitch), and which words are at the bottom of the tone 'valleys' (lower in pitch).

Continue comparing English and Russian contours and their placement and purposes in sentences. Just remember, as you listen to native speakers, pay attention to which words are on the top of the tone curve, and which are relaxed into the valleys. Imagine you are listening to musical patterns.

These patterns of word placement and intonation patterns in English are predictable for a reason. They allow listeners to predict what you mean and what's most important. This makes it possible for listeners to keep pace with your idea and intention, rather than having to mentally process every single word you say. Instead, they are hearing whole phrases. They are identifying a question and its type, right from the start.

SUMMARY

- *Intonation* is a *really big deal* to native English speakers. As hard as it is to change something you don't think about when you speak in Russian, you've got to learn to use the English patterns, especially for questions. If you're conversing with native English speakers, this can definitely affect their perceptions of your attitude, intentions and social skills.
- Even though Russian and English are both tonal languages, they apply tone and pitch changes differently. Learn the formulas.
- Russian Wh- questions spike in pitch at the beginning and then drop strongly. This pattern gives a negative impression if you use it in English. English Wh- patterns rise on the Wh- word and rise again on the most important noun or verb.
- Russian Yes/No questions spike strongly at the start and their contour drops continually, but in English it's the reverse: they start lower and rise in tone all the way to the final focus word.

Practice these consciously and revisit them occasionally or you will fall back to your unconscious Russian habits.

---

1. Crosby, Christiane Fleur, "L1 Influence on L2 Intonation in Russian Speakers of English" (2013). *Dissertations and Theses.* Paper 1070.
   https://pdxscholar.library.pdx.edu/open_access_etds/1070
   10.15760/etd.1070

   If you type her name *Crosby, Christiane Fleur* into your search bar, her thesis paper will come up.

22

▶ ▶ QUESTION INTONATIONS

WHAT WORKS IN RUSSIAN DOESN'T WORK IN ENGLISH

YOU MUST CHANGE the *way* you ask questions. English uses specific, prescribed intonation patterns for Wh-questions (who, what, when, where, why, how) and for Yes/No questions. So does Russian. Too bad they're not the same. Do you remember the graph I showed you that compared question intonation patterns in Russian and English? We are going to work on your English question intonations now. Don't forget that you will also need to give individual words more stress if they are important, no matter which intonation pattern you are practicing, Wh- or Yes/No.

WH- QUESTIONS

In Russian, a Wh-question has a sharp spike at the beginning to stress the Wh-word, with the rest of the question dropping tonally to your lowest pitch. You saw that in the graphs.

But it's exactly the opposite in English. Using this normal Russian intonation pattern will make you sound negative in English—perhaps harsh, mean, grumpy, angry, doubtful, apathetic—something not so nice, not so friendly.

To make sure you don't confuse or alienate people, change the intonation contour you use for English questions. Start your question just below or at mid-range and end your question above your middle pitch. The end should be the highest pitch point in your sentence, and just at the end, at the last syllable of the final content word, drop your pitch a bit.

Look at the following image—see the small downward movement at the end of both questions? The first has a small drop; the second has a bigger drop. **How far you drop depends on the person and the moment.** But what's **not negotiable** is this: you must have a higher ending followed by a drop. You **must** do this when you ask a WH- question.

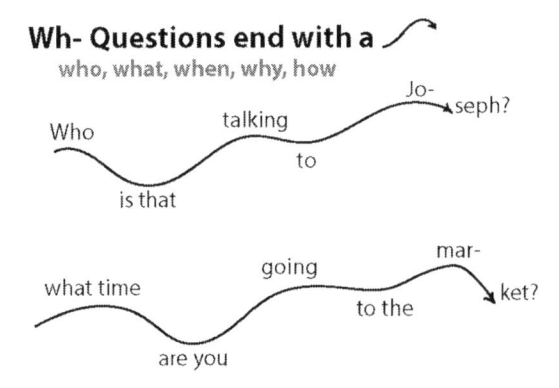

Wh- Questions end with a ⌒
who, what, when, why, how

Who is that talking to Jo-seph?

what time are you going to the mar-ket?

Below is a list of questions to practice. Say them moving steadily upward in pitch, accentuating your important words, ending with your last word at the highest level. If the word is a 2 syllable word, like *doing*, do- will be the highest point in your sentence and -ing will drop down at the end.

If the last word has only 1 syllable, like *from* or *is*, start the word at your highest pitch, then bend the vowel downward in pitch as you say it, so that you have the downward hook.

If the last words make up a compound noun, like *dentist's office* or *White House*, the first word reaches up and the second word drops a bit.

It's the same for a verb + adverb like *get there*. *Get* is higher; *there* slides down. In general, any final supporting words or phrases can drop together: *for it, on it, of it*. Listen to native speakers when they ask questions, or ask an American friend to say some for you. You'll hear that the drop happens in the easiest-to-understand place.

Say these Wh-questions. **Bolded** words get primary stress, *italicized* words may or may not have secondary stress, depending on what you are asking about. Final underlined words have the highest tone in the sentence, with a rise-then-fall in pitch.

What are you **do**ing?

Who do you *think* it **is**?

Where are *they* **from**?

When did you *see* her **last**?

How are we going to **get** *there*?

Why didn't you *tell* me this **earli**er?

YES-NO QUESTIONS

Take another look at the Yes/No question graph in the previous chapter.

In Russian, your voice rises sharply on the stressed syllable of the focus word, has a short downward hook at the top, then returns to the continuous low tones. But in English, your question starts low and rises up in waves until the last word. Try to get more modulation, more wave movement in your phrases, by focusing on important words.

You're going on vacation?   Yes/no Question   ↗

Say the following yes/no questions, giving **bolded** words primary stress, *italicized* words secondary stress, and end with a continuous rise upward on the underlined words. End above your mid-range.

Are you *going* to the **doctor**?

Is *this* your new **home**?

Will they *be here* in time to see the **movie**?

COMBINING PATTERNS

We're going to combine questions and statements so you can get stronger at using the right intonation contours at the right time.

You're going on vacation?   Yes/no Question   ↗

Where?   Wh- Question   ↗⤵

When are you leaving?   Wh-Question   ↗⤵

Call me when you get back.   Statement   ↘

PRACTICE

Drill these sets of sentences until you can easily change, back and forth, from WH-question intonation to YES/NO question intonation to statement intonation. This is something you will need to do in real life. When you've finished practicing these, change the words and create your own sentences. Mix up the order you say them in.

<u>*Italicized* words get secondary stress. **Bolded** words get primary stress. Don't forget to use the appropriate final tone movement.</u>

You're *going* on **vacation**?

Where?

When are you **leaving**?

Are you **renting** your *house* out while you're **gone**?

Call me when you get **back**.

* * *

How's the **weather**?

Do you think I'll *need* a **raincoat**?

I've got an **umbrella** in the car if you *need* one.

* * *

Why are they selling their **home**?

I'd **love** to *live* there.

How much are they **asking** for it?

Have you *seen* the **inside**?

* * *

Who's the **woman** standing *next to* Larissa?

I *think* it's our new **mayor**.

She seems **young**. How **old** do you think she is?

I *don't know* but I hope she does a **good job**.

KEEP LISTENING

Find your favorite TV or movie characters and look for some normal conversations. But remember, comedians use more extremes, a very wide range of tone, much more movement with higher and lower pitches...they do this to entertain us. These are great to start with because they're easy to hear. The TV show 'Friends' is a good example of comedic use of voices in English.

If you're not too tired of playphrase.me yet, type in a question, then get a piece of paper and draw the intonation curves as you listen to each video clip.

Your job is to be familiar with movements like these and learn when to use them. So be observant, listen, imitate, experiment, and think about the differences between normal speakers and actors.

SUMMARY

- If you are using Russian intonation contours when you speak English, you definitely don't sound like a native speaker of English. Practice English intonation. It's important.
- English WH-questions (who, what, when, where, why, how) have their highest pitch on the last word, which then drops on the last syllable. This final rise + drop is a *required* form for WH questions. Russian questions have much different contour.
- Our Yes/No questions also have very different sounds. Russian Y/N questions have high stress with a hook to the

focus word and the remainder of the question moving along at a steady low pitch. But English Y/N questions start at mid or lower and then gradually rise with the focus words until the question's highest pitch on the last word. There is <u>no</u> drop in pitch at the end.

23

▶ ▶ EXCLAMATIONS AND SHORT RESPONSES 🎧

USING RUSSIAN INTONATION IN ENGLISH

LET'S talk about English and Russian speaking ranges—the span between the lowest and highest tones used in Russian and English. To start with, speak as low as you comfortably do, and then gradually raise your tones higher and higher until you arrive at your own highest speech tone. Now divide that span into 4 levels of tones, so we can talk about how you use can your range of sounds as Americans do. If you don't do this, it won't be possible to follow the practice exercises later, so stop now and play around with your voice, finding 4 levels of tone in your speaking range. Name them 1, for lowest, 2 for low middle, 3 for high middle, and 4.0 for highest normal speaking (not screaming or yelling).

PLEASE NOTE: These 4 divisions are an artificial construct so you and I can discuss English and Russian tone use. Native speakers are not aware of this idea and if you asked them, they would have no idea what you were talking about. If asked, they might describe their speech as 'moving up and down a bit sometimes', if they are aware of tone movement at all. Since we learned tone use as babies, it's not a conscious habit for most people.

3.5 is for **key** words, **new** ideas or a **change** in topic.

2.5 —3.0, the middle ranges, are intonation curves with supporting **content** words that form the basis of your message.

1.5—2.0 is for grammatical words such as prepositions (of, to, in) and articles (the, those), pronouns (he, she, it) and any content that has already been discussed in the conversation.

1.0 is for closure, for ending ideas, for changing topics, or to signal to conversational partners that you are finished and it's their turn to speak. Most English speakers, but not all, take turns in conversations or use these falling tones to help others know when they can jump in.

* * *

4.0, your highest natural speech tone, is reserved for extreme expressions only. Ironically, this high tone is used often in Russian for normal, everyday speech, with dramatic jumps and drops from this high position to Russian's naturally low tones. In Russian, 4.0 sounds neutral, even formal. But if you use 4.0 in English, that statement will probably not be thought of as neutral at all.

Here are some ways English speakers *do* use 4.0. Note that these expressions are not 'neutral' or 'formal'. 4.0 is used in English for highly *reactive* expressions, for strongly *pessimistic* statements, to express *anger* or *frustration*, or used for *over-emoting*, i.e. speaking with *exaggerated* enthusiasm.

In the examples below, level **4.0 words** are in **bold**. If you use your comfortable Russian 4.0 stress tone, you may be communicating the emotion described in the parentheses below.

EXAMPLES OF TONE 4.0 USE IN ENGLISH

Oh my **gosh**! 3-1-4 (strong reaction of surprise)

Help me! 4-1 or 4-2 or 4-3 (cry for help)

No! The **oth**er one! 4-2-4-2-1 (strong insistence)

Stop! 4 (urgent command)

Stop! 4-1 (command with insistence)

I **ser**iously **doubt** that. 2-4-2-1-1-4-1 (strong pessimism)

It's **so wonderful** to **see** you! 2-4-4-4-4-2-4-1 (strongly effusive)

PRACTICE 1

Say the above phrases with 4.0 tone so you know what a *strong reaction* should sound like in English. Give the phrases energy and volume, and spike your pitch up to your highest comfortable tone.

Now let's practice the same phrases with less intensity. This will sound more like most native speakers in a calm, friendly conversation. Say them less strongly. Use a 3.0 tone on the bolded word, so you know how it should feel to express a *mild reaction* or normal communicative stress. Smooth out the ups and downs. Remember, this is where you want to "live" when you speak English—gliding up and down in the 2's and 3's (not the 1's and 4's).

PRACTICE 2

Here's another tone pattern that is used differently in Russian and English. In Russian, the pitch pattern 2-3-1 is used for announcements, proclamations, formal reading and speaking; it's an emotionally neutral pattern in Russian.

But in English, it tonally expresses a negative reaction and English listeners have an immediate impression of negativity when they hear you use this pattern. Here are 3 examples.

> I don't care! (apathy) 2-3-1—
> You're kidding! (sarcasm) 2-3-1—
> Unbelievable! (disapproval) 2-3-3-1-1—

If you forget and use this 2-3-1 pattern in a short statement, your

English listeners will automatically assume you are feeling less than enthusiastic about your topic.

ARE YOU FRIENDLY? SERIOUS? ANGRY? NEUTRAL? TELL US WITH YOUR TONE.

We native speakers often talk about a person's *tone* because it has a strong effect on us. It signals mood, intentions, needs, expectations. If a child speaks disrespectfully to his parents, they will chastise him, saying "Don't use that tone of voice with me!" A person might observe "He seemed angry—did you get that from his tone?" or "That was rude; I don't like her tone."

How do we use tone to express our attitude or feeling toward another other person? If someone narrows their speaking range and speaks only in the zone of level 2 and level 1, they sound either serious, negative, apathetic or bored—their words will finish telling us which attitude it is.

If you're happy, stay around levels 2 - 3.5, going up to 3 or 3.5 for your focus words, and dropping to 2 for the rest. And smile! It may not feel natural, but if you want Americans to be receptive to you and trust you, smile a little and speak in the 'happy 2.5–3.5 zone', especially when you first meet. Once you get to know each other, you can stop grinning all the time, but you will make more friends by speaking in the happy zones and looking friendly and open.

Remember, to convey emotions or attitudes, serious is low, bored is low, agitated is high, excited is high. Normal lives in the middle zones.

PRACTICE 3

Let's have some fun. Go to playphrase.me and put in the following bulleted phrases below, one by one, and listen to the video clips. You'll notice that the tone movement, the "musical notes" that English speakers use form a predictable musical "phrase". Just about every person follows the same tonal pattern. Analyze the change in musical notes—which word is lowest, and which is highest. Notice which word is longest and strongest, and think about why. In the last example below, *nope*, some speakers actually change the pitch of the vowel as they say it; the word often starts on a higher note and ends slightly lower.

Warning #1: these clips are taken from actual movies, so there may be scenes or words that are a bit risqué.

Warning #2: Don't say these in formal situations! These are only for close friends and informal conversations.

- oh my god
- what the hell happened here
- what the heck
- oh crap
- yes, I do
- you've got to be kidding me
- nope

PRACTICE 4

Find a TV series or movie you like to watch. Listen for the speakers' tone and pitch movement. Have the following questions in front of you to remind yourself what to listen for. Once you recognize these acoustic strategies, you *must* starting using them if you want to sound natural in English.

1. If you hear someone's voice jump to 4 quickly and energetically, ask yourself—are they excited, upset, surprised? Something dramatic is going on.
2. Does someone end on a 1, pause briefly, then jump pitch to a 3 in order to change the direction of the topic?
3. Listen for times when speakers keep their tone changes restricted to 2 and 1. Are they being serious? Are they worried? Apathetic? Bored?
4. Listen for times when voices roll over tonal hills and valleys

in the 3 and 2 ranges—are they calm, content, happy? What is happening in that scene? Use a modulating series of tonal hills and valleys that slide up the tonal hills on meaningful words and glide down to the tonal valleys for less important words.

5. Listen for times when TV characters emphasize specific words. How did they do that? Were they louder? Or slower? Practice emphasizing unique nouns, verbs, adverbs and adjectives in your own messages, the words that carry the important, new parts of your message.

SUMMARY

- English uses a wider range of tone than Russian so you must get comfortable using a lot more of your middle ranges to create smooth (not abrupt) movements in tone. Abrupt, large jumps and falls (1 to 4, or 4 to 1) sound strident and terse in English, so save them for when you are feeling that way. If you're feeling irritated or angry, show this by leaping up and drop down sharply on one important word. If you're feeling insistent but not angry, do it more gently, less sharply.
- Use 3's and 2's the most, and save 1's for your final endings. Starting at your natural mid-pitch, use 3.5 for most important words, 1.5 for function words (like *to, a, for, at, the, he, she*) and stay in 2.5—3 range for most of your message. Create gentle *hillsides and valleys* of sound as you highlight your stressed words.
- Stress only one or two words in a statement or question (unless you're screaming). Your focus words should sit at the top of their own intonation hill. Decide which of the important words is the **theme** word and make it your key word.

24

PITCH RESETS 🎧

AN EASY COMMUNICATION SIGNAL THAT HELPS YOUR LISTENERS STAY CONNECTED TO YOUR IDEA CHANGES

THE LAST STRATEGY I'm going to leave you with is something quite easy to learn and use!

Here's a metaphor to get the idea. In the United States, we call our cars' external turn indicator lights *'turn signals'*. In Great Britain, they're called indicator lights. Their purpose is to signal a change in direction. They tell others which way we are going.

English speech has the pronunciation equivalent to this 'change in direction' signal. I call this *'pitch reset'*. A *pitch reset* is a simple way for you to signal to listeners that you are going to change topic or go off in another direction. All native English speakers do this naturally. It helps to prevent confusion in the conversation.

Paragraph indentations do the same in written language. They signal the start of a new idea, or a new perspective, just as pitch resets do in speech.

If something you are going to say is the start of a new idea or a new topic, or a change in your attitude to it, briefly pause before starting to speak again, and then jump your pitch up to above middle range on the start of the new idea. This sudden pitch jump follows your previous low-pitch signal that the previous statement is finished.

Don't go as high in pitch as your highest pitch in Russian; no 4's please! This new-info pitch level is about a 3 or 3.5 at the highest; it's above your middle range, but not your highest.

Pitch reset tells you listeners that this is the start of a new idea, a turn of some sort, or a change in focus. It allows your listeners to stay with the flow of your thoughts and the changes in your thinking.

Do you read music? This is how pitch reset looks on a musical staff.

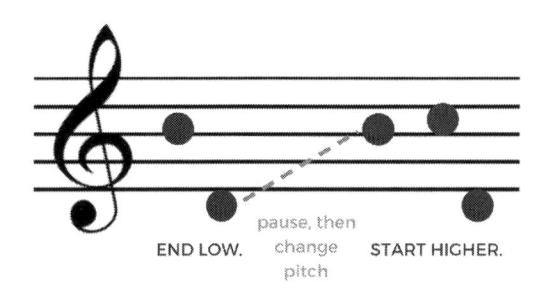

You can see the first statement drops in pitch on the final word *low*. There's a pause (a good time to breathe), then a jump in pitch on the first word of the next sentence: *start*. If the first word had been *the, a, for, in*, or any content-poor word, your pitch would have stayed low after the pause and jumped on the first focus word. Since this sentence begins with the verb *start*, the pitch jump happened immediately on that content-rich word.

This pattern, [end low>brief pause>start higher], signals that you are changing the topic or direction of your message in some way. **The longer the pause and higher the pitch jump, the bigger the change of topic.**

Use pitch resets the way you would use paragraph indentations if you were writing—to signal new important information or a change or turn in the topic.

And the bonus for you as a Russian speaker is this: using pitch resets will help you explore your middle speaking range more, which will reduce your accent and make you sound more like a native English speaker.

PRACTICE 1

Let's practice listening for smaller pitch resets in the middle of statements. These are more subtle, but still inform your listeners about the direction and connection of your ideas. Go to playphrase.me and type this:

it, why

Tune up your ears and listen hard for the drop in pitch on "it" and the reset rise on "why". The drop signals the end of one phrase, the reset signals the beginning of a new one. You must learn to recognize resets when other people are speaking, and recognize what they signal, in the same way that you recognize what a comma signifies when you are reading.

And you must learn to use them yourself, so imitate these examples, noticing how the mood and situation of the speakers affects the reset.

Once you know about pitch reset, you'll be amazed to hear it all the time. Start using it! You'll be on your way to sounding much more like a native English speaker.

PRACTICE 2

Go back to Train Your Accent and listen to the recorded paragraphs again. Listen to *everything*: his reduced vowels in function words, his pitch reset to signal new starts, how he stresses important theme and focus words.

And if he's still too fast to keep up with, don't worry. I find him annoyingly fast. But some people really do talk this quickly. I hope you are now noticing more of his signals.

Rest assured, not everyone speaks at that fast pace, so if you'd prefer different practice materials, use a video with conversations and listen for pitch resets. Listen to how speakers signal to listeners using stress, pitch resets, and falling tones—the speaker is trying hard to help you follow the flow of their idea.

PRACTICE 3

Open up a podcast that you like to listen to, and start paying attention to the tone signals when the conversation changes or speakers change. Interviews and co-hosted podcasts are good for this because the speakers can't see each other, and must signal to each other and collaborate to move the conversation forward. You will hear a significant jump in pitch as new topics come up. You'll hear pitch reset when one person stops and the next person begins with their message. Stop now, and do this listening exercise. You must learn when and how to use pitch resets in your own speech, so pay attention, and then try it out when you are speaking with friends or colleagues.

SUMMARY

- To use a pitch reset, drop to your lowest comfortable speaking pitch at the end of the previous sentence to signal closure. Then jump up in pitch on the first *meaningful* word of your next statement (not on *the, for, to*, etc. but the noun or verb that defines your new idea).
- Reset your pitch to mid-range or higher when you are changing direction in the conversation or starting something new. Combined with pauses, pitch reset tells your listeners a lot.
- Longer pauses with greater pitch resets tell listeners that the change will be big. Short (or no) pauses and small resets say that you are going to add something new but it is tied to the previous statement.

PART 5 WELL DONE!

Great job! You are amazing! Now you know the strategies and techniques that will help you improve your sound in English.

It's crucial that you continue with the practices and exercises so you can maintain your new American sounds and tones. Keep studying native speakers on TV and YouTube, and don't forget about PlayPhrase.me. Keep listening!

I'm honored, amazed, and relieved that you made it all the way to the end! It's been a lot, I know, but you don't have to master all of it at once. Work on one strategy at a time. Your English sound *will* improve as these sounds become habitual and your speech muscles get more comfortable with the sounds and movements of English.

With all my heart, I wish you good luck and success in future.

До скорой встречи!

Peggy Tharpe

If you need me, you can find me on YouTube, Facebook, Twitter, Udemy, at AmericanPronunciationCoach.com, my website, or just search for my name online.

MESSAGE FROM PEGGY

Did you like it?
Did it help?
Was it just right?
Was it too much?
Please tell me.

If you found this guide helpful, I'd be very grateful if you would leave a review. Your opinion matters hugely to me, and even more so to readers who are wondering if they should take a chance on my book. To leave a review, search my name in the online store where you found it—my titles will pop up for you. Thank you so very much.

However…if you *didn't* find it helpful, please email me directly at peggy@americanpronunciationcoach.com and tell me why so I can learn from your experience and viewpoint. My goal is to make the best resource and teaching guides possible. Thanks.

STAY IN TOUCH

I look forward to seeing you again. If you would like to stay in touch by receiving occasional newsletters with tips, strategies, announcements and coupons, sign up here.

ALSO BY PEGGY THARPE

Available at online bookstores and Amazon:

English Pronunciation, Intonation and Speaking Fluency for **JAPANESE** *Speakers*

English Pronunciation, Intonation and Speaking Fluency for **ARABIC** *Speakers*

TESL, TEFL, How to **Teach English Vowel Sounds** *for Mastery*, on Udemy.com

* * *

HERE'S THE URL AND PASSWORD YOU NEED FOR THE LINKS AND RECORDINGS IN THIS BOOK:

URL

http://AmericanPronunciationCoach.com/russian

(be careful of your typing and use this American spelling of pronunciation, not the British spelling)

PASSWORD: 4603

If you have problems accessing the webpage, contact me at peggy@AmericanPronunciationCoach.com This is only for people who have purchased the book.

ABOUT THE AUTHOR

PEGGY THARPE is the person behind the books, online courses, videos, and her website, American Pronunciation Coach.com. Her career grew out of her love of music, speech and languages. She's a 'lifer' in the world of ESL, EFL, ELL and ELT and has taught around the world in public and private institutions, working with all ages, from young children to corporate leaders. She trains teachers and coaches students privately, sometimes speaks at conferences, and is continually writing books, creates courses, and doing whatever she can to help people become stronger and more confident at teaching and learning the sound of English. To find out more about her background and career, read Peggy's resume, and find her online.

Printed in Great Britain
by Amazon